In Sheep's Clothing

Understanding and Dealing with Manipulative People

"After having read several books on several different self-help topics, psychology books, psychiatry books, etc., I MUST recommend you buy this one, first. It cuts straight through the bs - neatly and cleanly. I have bought copies of this book for friends and can't recommend it enough."

—E. Adams, Online Purchaser

"Don't Be Bossed-Around Ever Again !!! ... *In Sheep's Clothing: Understanding and Dealing with Manipulative People* by George K. Simon, Jr., Ph.D., is a godsend to anyone who has ever questioned their own sanity while in any kind of relationship with a controlling and manipulative person.

—The Aeolian Kid, Online Purchaser

"Dr. Simon teaches the mechanics of popular tactics used by manipulators and how you can identify and thwart their attacks so that you control the outcome. This book helped me with a person that I have no choice but to see daily. After the end of every "friendly" conversation I felt depressed or insulted but could not figure out how this person was doing it. This book helped me to understand what was really happening. Dr. Simon's guidelines exposed this person and [allowed me to take] control. Because this person knows [I] can no longer [be] controlled, I now have—not a perfect relationship—but one that's better than the alternative."

—A reader in Chicago

"This book is like the secret decoder ring for the jumbled mess that is a manipulator's modus operandi. **Do yourself a favor and get this book now.**"

—Christy, Missouri

"It's sad that there are people out there that make life so much harder than it should have to be for others. Being able to identify such people in your life (both at home and at work) is very important and can be of invaluable help to 1) not go crazy oneself, and 2) take corrective action. Dr. Simon's book is written with amazing clarity. **If you read only one book this year, read this one.**"

—JA008, Online Purchaser

"This is one of the best books I've ever read and **I would recommend it to anyone.** It has redefined how I judge people and helped me to become a stronger person. I used to be very naive and unaware of people's ulterior motives, and I have learned a tremendous amount from reading this book."

—S. Brescenti, Online Purchaser

"This book makes it clear that evil is allowed free rein because of our ignorance of its nature. Simon shows us what seemingly mundane interactions that leave us perplexed may really be about. According to him, master manipulators leave us drained and confused as we try to change them into the good person we want to believe they really are. I would add that the manipulators are just plain evil because evil requires lies, manipulation and a weakening of the other's will through deception. Simon shows you how to recognize the signs and what you can do about it. Good people are responsible for informing and protecting themselves from the manipulators in society. This book is a necessary start."

—Kaye, a reader in New York state

"Pithy and often funny, George Simon takes the bluster and obfuscation of overbearing, weaselly bosses, nasty neighbors, and obnoxious coworkers and boils it down to show you the simple psychological strategies being used to impose on your patience, good will, or even wallet. **I have recommended this book to everyone I know and bought extra copies for my kids** when they went out into the work world. Highly Recommended!"

—C. MacCallum, Online Purchaser

In Sheep's Clothing

Understanding and Dealing with Manipulative People

George K. Simon, Jr., Ph.D.

Parkhurst Brothers, Inc., Publishers
LITTLE ROCK

www.parkhurstbrothers.com

A.J. Christopher printing history: First printing, November 1996; Eleventh Printing, September 2009.
A. J. Christopher edition is out-of-print effective 3.31.2010 by agreement with Parkhurst Brothers, Inc., Publishers, whose edition is available as of 4.1.2010.

2022   16 15 14 13 12 11 10 9 8 7 6

PARKHURST BROTHERS paperback edition ISBN 978-1-935166-30-6

PARKHURST BROTHERS ebook edition ISBN 978-1-935166-31-3

Library of Congress cataloging reference information is available on the publisher's
website pages for this title. Please consult www.parkhurstbrothers.com for the information.

www.parkhurstbrothers.com

ACKNOWLEDGMENTS

I am deeply grateful to my wife, Dr. Sherry Simon for her unfailing love, faith, understanding, patience, and support. She is responsible for the title of this book and was a valuable resource in helping me clarify my thoughts during its writing.

I wish to thank Dr. Bruce Carruth for his critique of the original manuscript and suggestions for making it more readable.

I am deeply indebted to the work of Dr. Theodore Millon. His comprehensive approach to understanding personality has not only influenced my thinking on the subject but also proved invaluable in my efforts to help people change.

I owe a supreme debt to the many individuals willing to share with me their experiences with manipulative people. They taught me much and enriched my life. This book, in large measure, is a tribute to their courage and support.

I am most appreciative of the validation, support, and enriching input consistently afforded me by workshop attendees. They have helped me clarify, refine, and enhance one of my principal missions in life.

Words cannot express the gratitude I have for the thousands of readers who have kept this book on the active lists of online booksellers and retail outlets for over 15 years. The many emails, blog posts, and letters readers have sent helped me make necessary updates and changes to this Revised Edition. I have attempted to honor the considerable feedback I continue to receive by expanding the discussion of key concepts as well as introducing important new content for this newly revised edition.

Finally, I want to thank Roger Armbrust and Ted Parkhurst of Parkhurst Brothers, Inc., Publishers. Ted encouraged me at the outset and was there when I needed him; Roger's grace and presence have only benefited my work and readers.

PREFACE

Whether it's the supervisor who claims to support you while thwarting every opportunity you have to get ahead, the co-worker who quietly undermines you to gain the boss's favor, the spouse who professes to love and care about you but seems to control your life, or the child who always seems to know just which buttons to push in order to get their way, manipulative people are like the proverbial wolf in sheep's clothing. On the surface they can appear charming and genial. But underneath, they can be ever so calculating and ruthless. Cunning and subtle, they prey on your weaknesses and use clever tactics to gain advantage over you. They're the kind of people who fight hard for everything they want but do their best to conceal their aggressive intentions. That's why I call them covert-aggressive personalities.

As a clinical psychologist in private practice, I began to focus on the problem of covert aggression over 20 years ago. I did so because the depression, anxiety, and feelings of insecurity that initially led several of my patients to seek help eventually turned out to be in some way linked to their relationship with a manipulative person. I've counseled not only the victims of covert-aggression, but also manipulators themselves experiencing distress because their usual ways of getting their needs met and controlling others weren't working anymore. My work has given me an appreciation for how widespread problem of manipulative behavior is and the unique emotional stress it can bring to a relationship.

The scope of the problem of covert-aggression seems self-evident. Most of us know at least one manipulative person. And hardly a day goes by that we don't read in the newspaper or hear a broadcast about someone who managed to exploit or "con" many before fate shed some light on their true character. There's the televangelist who preached love, honesty, and decency while cheating on his wife and fleecing his flock, the politician, sworn to "public service," caught lining his pockets, or the spiritual "guru" who even managed to convince most of his followers that he was God incarnate while sexually exploiting their children and subtly terrorizing those who challenged him. The world, it seems full of manipulators.

Although the extreme wolves in sheep's clothing that make headlines grab our attention and pique our curiosity about what makes such people "tick," most of the covertly aggressive people we are likely to encounter are not these larger-than-life characters. Rather, they are the subtly underhanded, backstabbing, deceptive, and conniving individuals we may work with, associate with, or possibly even live with. And they can make life miserable. They cause us grief because we find it so hard to truly understand them and even harder to deal with them effectively.

When victims of covert-aggression first seek help for their emotional distress, they usually have little insight into why they feel so bad. They only know that they feel confused, anxious, or depressed. Gradually, however, they relate how dealing with a certain person in their lives makes them feel crazy. They don't really trust them but can't pinpoint why. They get mad at them but for some reason end up feeling guilty themselves. They confront them about their behavior, only to wind up on the defensive. They get frustrated because they find themselves frequently giving in when they really wanted to stand ground, saying "yes" when they mean to say "no," and becoming depressed because nothing they try seems to make things better. In the end, dealing with this person always leaves them feeling confused, exploited and abused. After exploring the issues in therapy for a while, they eventually come to realize how much of their unhappiness is the direct result of their constant but fruitless attempts to understand, deal with, or control their manipulator's behavior.

Despite the fact that many of my patients are intelligent, resourceful individuals with a fair understanding of traditional psychological principles, most of the ways they tried to understand and cope with their manipulator's behavior weren't getting them anywhere, and some of the things they tried only seemed to make matters worse. Moreover, none of the ways that I initially tried to help made any real difference. Having an eclectic training background, I tried all sorts of different therapies and strategies, all of which seemed to help the victims feel a little better, but none seemed to empower them enough to really change the nature of their relationship with their manipulator. Even more disconcerting was the fact that none of the approaches I tried was effective at all with the manipulators. Realizing that something must be fundamentally wrong with the traditional approaches to understanding and dealing with manipulative people, I began to carefully study the problem in the hope of developing a practical, more effective approach.

In this book I would like to introduce you to a new way of

understanding the character of manipulative people. I believe the perspective I will offer describes manipulators and labels their behavior more accurately than many other approaches. I'll explain what covert-aggression is and why I believe it's at the heart of most interpersonal manipulation. I'll focus some needed attention on dimensions of personality that are too often ignored by traditional perspectives. The framework I will be advancing challenges some of the more common assumptions we make about why people act the way they do and explains why some of the most widely-held beliefs about human nature tend to set us up for victimization by manipulators.

I have three objectives to fulfill in this book. My first is to fully acquaint you the nature of disturbed characters as well as the distinctive character of the covertly aggressive personality. I'll discuss the characteristics of aggressive personality types in general and outline the unique characteristics of the covert-aggressive personality. I'll present several vignettes, based on real cases and situations, that will help you get the "flavor" of this personality type as well as illustrate how manipulative people operate. Being able to recognize a wolf in sheep's clothing and knowing what to expect from this kind of person is the first step in avoiding being victimized by them.

My second objective is to explain precisely how covertly aggressive people manage to deceive, manipulate, and "control" others. Aggressive and covertly aggressive people use a select group of interpersonal maneuvers or tactics to gain advantage over others. Becoming more familiar with these tactics really helps a person recognize manipulative behavior at the time it occurs, and makes it easier, therefore, to avoid being victimized. I'll also discuss the characteristics many of us possess that can make us unduly vulnerable to the tactics of manipulation. Knowing what aspects of your own character a manipulator is most likely to exploit is another important step in avoiding victimization.

My final objective is to outline the specific steps anyone can take to deal more effectively with aggressive and covertly aggressive personalities. I'll present some general rules for redefining the rules of engagement with these kinds of individuals and describe some specific tools of personal empowerment that can help a person break the self-defeating cycle of trying to control their manipulator and becoming depressed in the process. Using these tools makes it more likely that a one-time victim will invest their energy where they really have power— in their own behavior. Knowing how to conduct yourself in a potentially manipulative encounter is crucial to becoming less vulnerable to a manipulator's ploys and asserting greater control over your own life.

I have attempted to write this book in a manner that is serious and substantial yet straightforward and readily understandable. I have written it for the general public as well as the mental health professional, and I hope both will find it useful. By adhering to many traditional assumptions, labeling schemes, and intervention strategies, therapists sometimes hold and inadvertently reinforce some of the same misconceptions that their patients harbor about the character and behavior of manipulators that inevitably lead to continued victimization. I offer a new perspective in the hope of helping individuals and therapists alike avoid enabling manipulative behavior.

AUTHOR'S NOTE ON THE REVISED EDITION

Since this book's first wide publication in 1996, I have received thousands of calls, letters, and emails, and heard countless testimonials and comments at workshops from individuals whose lives were changed merely by being exposed to and adopting a new perspective on understanding human behavior. A common theme voiced by readers and workshop attendees is that once they dispelled old myths and came to view problem behaviors in a different light, they could see clearly that what their intuition had told them all along was correct, and thus felt validated. A similar phenomenon has held true for mental health professionals attending the many training seminars I have given. Once they abandoned their old notions about why their clients do the things they do, they were better able to help them and their significant others. I had already been doing workshops for 10 years before writing *In Sheep's Clothing*. At that time, only a handful of theorists, researchers, and writers were recognizing the need for a new perspective on understanding and dealing with disturbed characters (e.g., Stanton Samenow, Samuel Yochelson, Robert Hare). What professionals today call the cognitive-behavioral approach was in its infancy. The early research on character disturbance inspired me and helped me validate my own observations. Today an increasing number of professionals are recognizing the problem of character disturbance and using cognitive-behavioral methods to diagnose and treat it.

We live in an age radically different from that in which the classical theories of psychology and personality were developed. For the most part, truly pathological degrees of neurosis are quite rare, and problematic levels of character disturbance are increasingly commonplace. It's a pervasive societal problem about which all of us would do well to expand our awareness. During the last 15 years, my experience working with disturbed characters of all types has grown immensely, as has the body of research. So, I have included in this edition an expanded discussion on the problem of character disturbance in general and what sets the disturbed character apart from your garden-variety neurotic.

I am deeply grateful for the excellent word-of-mouth support responsible for transforming a once small, independent work into a bestseller enjoying ever-increasing popularity even after nearly 20 years. I sincerely hope this revised edition will provide you with all the information and tools you need to better understand and deal with the manipulative people in your life.

George K. Simon, Jr., Ph.D.
September, 2014

TABLE OF CONTENTS

PART I

Understanding Manipulative Personalities

COVERT-AGGRESSION: THE HEART OF MANIPULATION

A Common Problem

Perhaps the following scenarios will sound familiar. A wife tries to sort out her mixed feelings. She's mad at her husband for insisting their daughter make all A's. But she doubts she has the right to be mad. When she suggested that given her appraisal of their daughter's abilities, he might be making unreasonable demands, his comeback, "Shouldn't *any* good parent want their child to do well and succeed in life?" made her feel like the insensitive one. In fact, whenever she confronts him, she somehow ends up feeling like the bad guy herself. When she suggested there might be more to her daughter's recent problems, and that the family might do well to seek counseling, his retort "Are you saying I'm psychiatrically disturbed?" made her feel guilty for bringing up the issue. She often tries to assert her point of view, but always ends up giving-in to his. Sometimes, she thinks the problem is him, believing him to be selfish, demanding, intimidating, and controlling. But this is a loyal husband, good provider, and a respected member of the community. By all rights she shouldn't resent him. Yet, she does. So, she constantly wonders if there isn't something wrong with her.

A mother tries desperately to understand her daughter's behavior. No young girl, she thought, would threaten to leave home, say things like "Everybody hates me" and "I wish I were never born," unless she were very insecure, afraid, and probably depressed. Part of her thinks her daughter is still the same child who used to hold her breath until she turned blue or threw tantrums whenever she didn't get her way. After all, it seems she only says and does these things when she's about to be disciplined or she's trying to get something she wants. But a part of her is afraid to believe that. "What if she really believes what she's saying?" she wonders. "What if I've really done something to hurt her and I just don't realize it?" she worries. She hates to feel "bullied" by her daughter's threats and emotional displays, but she can't take the chance her daughter might really be hurting—can she? Besides, children just don't act this way unless they really feel insecure or threatened in some way underneath it all—do they?

The Heart of the Problem

Neither victim in the preceding scenarios trusted their "gut" feelings. Unconsciously, they felt on the defensive, but consciously they had trouble seeing their manipulator as merely a person on the offensive. On one hand, they felt like the other person was trying to get the better of them. On the other, they found no objective evidence at the time to back-up their gut-level hunch. They ended up feeling crazy.

They're not crazy. The fact is, people fight almost all the time. And manipulative people are expert at fighting in subtle and almost undetectable ways. Most of the time, when they're trying to take advantage or gain the upper hand, you don't even know you're in a fight until you're well on your way to losing. When you're being manipulated, chances are someone is fighting with you for position, advantage, or gain, but in a way that's difficult to readily see. Covert-aggression is at the heart of most manipulation.

The Nature of Human Aggression

Our instinct to fight is a close cousin of our survival instinct.[1] Most everyone "fights" to survive and prosper, and *most* of the fighting we do is neither physically violent nor inherently destructive. Some theorists have suggested that only when this most basic instinct is severely frustrated does our aggressive drive have the potential to be expressed violently.[2] Others have suggested that some rare individuals seem to be predisposed to aggression—even violent aggression, despite the most benign circumstances. But whether extraordinary stressors, genetic predispositions, rein-forced learning patterns, or some combination of these are at the root of violent aggression, most theorists agree that aggression per se and destructive violence are not synonymous. In this book, the term aggression will refer to the forceful energy we all expend in our daily bids to survive, advance ourselves, secure things we believe will bring us some kind of pleasure, and remove obstacles to those ends.

People do a lot more fighting in their daily lives than we have ever been willing to acknowledge. The urge to fight is fundamental and instinctual. Anyone who denies the instinctual nature of aggression has either never witnessed two toddlers struggling for possession of the same toy, or has somehow forgotten this archetypal scene. Fighting is a big part of our culture, also. From the fierce partisan wrangling that characterizes representative government, to the competitive corporate environment, to the adversarial system of our judicial system, much fighting is woven into our societal fabric. We sue one another, divorce each other, battle with one another over our children, compete for jobs, and struggle with each other to advance certain goals, values, beliefs and ideals. The psychodynamic theorist Alfred Adler noted many years ago that we also forcefully strive to assert a sense of social superiority.[3] Fighting for personal and social advantage, we jockey with one another for power, prestige, and a secure social "niche." Indeed, we do so much fighting in so many aspects of our lives I think it fair to say that when human beings aren't making some kind of love, they're likely to be waging some kind of war.

Fighting is not inherently wrong or harmful. Fighting openly and fairly for our legitimate needs is often necessary and constructive. When we fight for what we truly need while respecting the rights and needs of others and taking care not to needlessly injure them, our behavior is best labeled *assertive*, and assertive behavior is one of the most healthy and necessary human behaviors. It's wonderful when we learn to assert ourselves in the pursuit of personal needs, overcome unhealthy dependency and become self-sufficient and capable. But when we fight unnecessarily, or with little concern about how others are being affected, our behavior is most appropriately labeled *aggressive*. In a civilized world, undisciplined fighting (aggression) is almost always a problem. The fact that we are an aggressive species doesn't make us inherently flawed or "evil," either. Adopting a perspective advanced largely by Carl Jung,[4] I would assert that the evil that sometimes arises from a person's aggressive behavior necessarily stems from his or her failure to "own" and discipline this most basic human instinct.

Two Important Types of Aggression

Two of the most fundamental types of fighting (others, such as reactive vs. predatory or instrumental aggression) will be discussed later are *overt* and *covert* aggression. When you're determined to have your way or gain advantage and you're open, direct, and obvious in your manner of fighting, your behavior is best labeled overtly aggressive. When you're out to "win," get your way, dominate, or control, but are subtle, underhanded, or deceptive enough to hide your true intentions, your behavior is most appropriately labeled covertly aggressive. Concealing overt displays of aggression while simultaneously intimidating others into backing-off, backing down, or giving-in is a very powerful manipulative maneuver. That's why *covert-aggression is most often the vehicle for interpersonal manipulation.*

Covert and Passive-Aggression

I often hear people say someone is being "passive-aggressive" when they're really trying to describe covertly aggressive behavior. Covert and passive-aggression are both indirect ways to aggress but they're most definitely not the same thing. Passive-aggression is, as the term implies, aggressing though passivity. Examples of passive-aggression are playing the game of emotional "get-back" with someone by resisting cooperation with them, giving them the "silent treatment," pouting or whining, not so accidentally "forgetting" something they wanted you to do because you're angry and didn't really feel like obliging them, etc. In contrast, covert aggression is very *active*, albeit veiled, aggression. When someone is being covertly aggressive, they're using calculating, underhanded means to get what they want or manipulate the response of others while keeping their aggressive intentions under cover.

Acts of Covert-Aggression vs. Covert-Aggressive Personalities

Most of us have engaged in some sort of covertly aggressive behavior from time to time but that doesn't necessarily make someone a covert-aggressive or manipulative personality. An individual's personality can be defined by the way he or she habitually perceives, relates to and interacts with others and the world at large.[5] It's the distinctive interactive "style" or relatively ingrained way a person prefers to deal with a wide variety of situations and to get the things they want in life. Certain personalities can be ever so ruthless in their interpersonal conduct while concealing their aggressive character or perhaps even projecting a convincing, superficial charm. These covert-aggressive personalities can have their way with you and look good in the process. They vary in their degree of ruthlessness and character pathology. But because the more extreme examples can teach us much about the process of manipulation in general, this book will pay special attention to some of the more seriously disturbed covert-aggressive personalities.

The Process of Victimization

For a long time, I wondered why manipulation victims have a hard time seeing what really goes on in manipulative interactions. At first, I was tempted to fault them. But I've learned that they get hoodwinked for some very good reasons:

1. A manipulator's aggression is not obvious. We might intuitively sense that they're trying to overcome us, gain power, or have their way, and find ourselves *unconsciously* intimidated. But because we can't point to clear, objective evidence they're aggressing against us, we can't readily validate our gut-level feelings.

2. The tactics that manipulators frequently use are powerful deception techniques that make it hard to recognize them as clever ploys. They can make it seem like the person using them is hurting, caring, defending, or almost anything but fighting for advantage over us. Their explanations always make just enough sense to make another doubt his or her gut hunch that they're being taken advantage of or abused. Their tactics not only make it hard for a person to consciously and objectively know their manipulator is fighting to overcome, but also simultaneously keep the victim unconsciously on the defensive. This makes the tactics highly effective psychological one-two punches. It's hard to think clearly when someone has you emotionally unnerved, so you're less likely to recognize the tactics for what they really are.

3. All of us have weaknesses and insecurities that a clever manipulator might exploit. Sometimes, we're aware of these weaknesses and how someone might use them to take advantage of us. For example, I hear parents say things like: "Yeah, I know I have a big guilt button." But at the time their manipulative child is busily pushing that button, they can easily forget what's really going on. Besides, sometimes we're unaware of our biggest vulnerabilities. Manipulators often know us better than we know ourselves. They know what buttons to push, when to do so and how hard to press. Our lack of self-awareness can easily set us up to be exploited.

4. What our intuition tells us a manipulator is really like challenges everything we've been taught to believe about human nature. We've been inundated with a psychology that has us viewing people with problems, at least to some degree, as afraid, insecure or "hung-up." So, while our gut tells us we're dealing with a ruthless conniver, our head tells us they must be really frightened, wounded, or self-doubting "under-neath." What's more, most of us generally hate to think of ourselves as callous and insensitive people. We hesitate to make harsh or negative judgments about others. We want to give them the benefit of the doubt and believe they don't really harbor the malevolent intentions we suspect. We're more apt to doubt and blame ourselves for daring to believe what our gut tells us about our manipulator's character.

Recognizing Aggressive Agendas

Accepting how fundamental it is for people to fight for

the things they want and becoming more aware of the subtle, under-handed ways people can and do fight in so many of their daily endeavors and relationships can be very consciousness-expanding. Learning to recognize an aggressive move when somebody makes one and learning how to handle oneself in any of life's many battles has turned out to be the most empowering experience for the manipulation victims with whom I've worked. It's how they eventually freed themselves from their manipulator's dominance and control and gained a much-needed boost to their own sense of self-esteem. Recognizing the inherent aggression in manipulative behavior and becoming more aware of the slick, surreptitious ways that manipulative people prefer to aggress against us is extremely important. Not recognizing and accurately labeling their subtly aggressive moves causes most people to misinterpret the behavior of manipulators and, therefore, fail to respond to them in an appropriate fashion. Recognizing when and how manipulators are fighting with you is fundamental to fairing well in any kind of encounter with them.

Unfortunately, mental health professionals and lay persons alike often fail to recognize the aggressive agendas and actions of others for what they really are. This is largely because we've been pre-programmed to believe that people only exhibit problem behaviors when they're "troubled" inside or anxious about something. We've also been taught that people aggress only when they're attacked in some way. So, even when our gut tells us that somebody is attacking us and for no good reason, or merely trying to overpower us, we don't readily accept the notions. We usually start to wonder what's bothering the person so badly "underneath it all" that's making them act in such a

23

disturbing way. We may even wonder what we may have said or done that "threatened" them. We may try to analyze the situation to death instead of simply responding to the attack. We almost never think that the person is simply fighting to get something they want, to have their way with us, or gain the upper hand. And, when we view them as primarily hurting in some way, we strive to understand as opposed to taking care of ourselves.

Not only do we often have trouble recognizing the ways people aggress, but we also have difficulty discerning the distinctly aggressive character of some personalities. The legacy of Sigmund Freud's work has a lot to do with this. Freud's theories (and the theories of others who expanded on his work) heavily influenced the field of psychology and related social sciences for a long time. The basic tenets of these classical (psychodynamic) theories and their hallmark construct, *neurosis*, have become fairly well etched in the public consciousness, and many psychodynamic terms have intruded into common parlance. These theories also tend to view *everyone,* at least to some degree, as *neurotic*. Neurotic individuals are overly inhibited people who suffer unreasonable and excessive anxiety (i.e. non-specific fear), guilt, and shame when it comes to acting on their basic instincts or trying to gratify their basic wants and needs. The malignant impact of over-generalizing Freud's observations about a small group of overly inhibited individuals into a broad set of assumptions about the causes of psychological ill-health in everyone cannot be overstated.[6] But these theories have so permeated our thinking about human nature, and especially our theories of personality, that when most of us try to analyze someone's character, we automatically start thinking in terms of what fears might be "hanging them up," what kinds of "defenses" they use and what kinds of psychologically "threatening" situations they may be trying to "avoid."

The Need for a New Psychological Perspective

Classical theories of personality were developed during an extremely repressive time. If there were a motto for the Victorian era, it would be: "Don't even think about it!" In such times, one would expect neurosis to be more prevalent. Freud treated individuals who were so riddled with excessive shame and guilt about their primal urges that some went "hysterically" blind so they wouldn't run the risk of consciously laying lustful eyes on the objects of their desire. Times have certainly changed. Today's social climate is far more permissive. If there were a motto for our time, it would be as the once popular TV commercial exhorted: "Just do it!" Many of the problems coming to the attention of mental health professionals these days are less the result of an individual's unreasonable fears and inhibitions and more the result of the deficient self-restraint a person has exercised over his/her basic instincts. More simply, therapists are increasingly being asked to treat individuals suffering from too little as opposed to too much neurosis (i.e. individuals with some type of *character disturbance*). As a result, classical theories of personality and their accompanying prescription for helping troubled persons achieve greater psychological health have proved to be of limited value when working with many of today's disturbed characters.

Some mental health professionals may need to overcome significant biases in order to better recognize and deal with aggressive or covertly aggressive behavior. Therapists who tend to see any kind of aggression not as a problem in itself but as a "symptom" of an underlying inadequacy, insecurity or unconscious fear, may focus so intently on their patient's supposed "inner conflict" that they overlook the aggressive behaviors most responsible for problems. Therapists whose training overly indoctrinated them in the theory of neurosis may "frame" the problems presented them incorrectly. They may, for example, assume that a person who all their life has aggressively pursued independence, resisted allegiance to others, and taken what they could from relationships without feeling obliged to give something back must necessarily be "compensating" for a "fear" of intimacy. In other words, they will view a hardened, abusive fighter as a terrified runner, thus misperceiving the core reality of the situation.

It's neither appropriate nor helpful to over-generalize the characteristics of neurotic personalities in the attempt to describe and understand all personalities. We need to stop trying to define *every* type of personality by their greatest fears of the principal ways they "defend" themselves. We need a completely different theoretical framework if we are to truly understand, deal with, and treat the kinds of people who fight too much as opposed to those who cower or "run" too much. I will present just such a framework in Chapter 1. I will introduce several aggressive personality types whose psychological makeup differs radically from those of the more neurotic personalities. It is within this framework that you will be better able to understand the nature of disturbed characters in general as well as the distinctive character of the manipulative people I call covert-aggressive personalities. I hope to present this new perspective not only in a style readily digestible by the lay reader trying to understand and cope with a difficult situation but also in a manner that should prove useful to mental health professionals attempting therapeutic interventions.

AGGRESSIVE AND COVERT-AGGRESSIVE PERSONALITIES

Understanding the true character of manipulative people is the first step in dealing more effectively with them. In order to know what they're really like, we have to view them within an appropriate context. In this chapter, I hope to present a framework for understanding personality and character that will help you distinguish manipulators from other personality types and give you an increased ability to identify a wolf in sheep's clothing when you encounter one.

Personality

The term personality derives from the Latin word "persona," which means "mask." In the ancient theater, when actors were only men, and when the art of conveying emotions through dramatic techniques had not fully evolved, female characters and various emotions were portrayed through the use of masks. Classical theorists, who conceptualized personality as the social façade or "mask" a person wore to hide the "true self," adopted the term. The classical definition of personality, however, has proven to be quite limiting.

Personality can also be defined as the unique manner that a person develops of perceiving, relating to and interacting with others and the world at large.[7] Within this model of personality, biology plays a part (e.g., genetic, hormonal influences, brain biochemistry), as does temperament, and of course, the nature of a person's environment and what he or she has learned from past experiences are big influences, also. All of these factors dynamically interact and contribute to the distinctive "style"[8] a person develops over time in dealing with others and coping with life's stressors in general. A person's interpersonal interactive "style" or personality appears a largely stable characteristic that doesn't moderate much with time and generalizes across a wide variety of situations.

Character

Everyone's unique style of relating to others has social, ethical and moral ramifications. The aspect of someone's personality that reflects how they accept and fulfill their social responsibilities and how they conduct themselves with others has sometime been referred to as *character*.[9] Some use the terms character and personality synonymously. But in this book, the term character will refer to those aspects of an individual's personality that reflect the extent to which they have developed personal integrity and a commitment to responsible social conduct. Persons of sound character temper their instinctual drives, moderate important aspects of their conduct, and especially, discipline their aggressive tendencies in the service of the greater social good.

Some Basic Personality Types

Volumes of clinical literature have been written on the various personality types. A discussion of all of the personality types is beyond the scope of this book. However, I find it particularly useful to distinguish between two basic dimensions of personality that occupy positions on opposite ends of a continuum that reflects how an individual deals with the challenges of life.

As goal-directed creatures, we all invest considerable time and energy trying to get the things we think will help us to prosper or bring us some kind of pleasure. Running into obstacles or barriers to what we want is the essence of human conflict. Now, there are fundamentally two things a person can do when running up against an obstacle to something they want. They can be so over-whelmed or intimidated by the resistance they encounter or so unsure of their ability to deal with it effectively, that they fearfully retreat. Alternatively, they can directly challenge the obstacle. If they are confident enough in their fighting ability and tenacious enough in their temperament, they might try to forcefully remove or overcome whatever stands between them and the object of their desire.

Submissive personalities *habitually* and *excessively* retreat from potential conflicts. They doubt their abilities and are excessively afraid to take a stand. Because they "run" from challenges too often, they deny themselves opportunities to experience success. This pattern makes it hard for them to develop a sense of personal competence and achieve self-reliance. Some personality theorists describe these individuals as *passive-dependent*[10] because their passivity largely leads them to become overly dependent upon others to do their fighting for them. Feeling inadequate, they all too readily submit to the will of those they view as more powerful or more capable than themselves.

In contrast, aggressive personalities are overly prone to fight in any potential conflict. Their main objective in life is "winning" and they pursue this objective with considerable passion. They forcefully strive to overcome, crush, or remove any barriers to what they want. They seek power ambitiously and use it unreservedly and unscrupulously when they get it. They always strive to be "on top" and in control. They accept challenges readily. Whether their faith in their ability to handle themselves in most conflicts is well-founded or not, they tend to be overly self-reliant or emotionally *independent*.

Neurotic and Character-Disordered Personalities

There are two other important dimensions of personality that represent opposite ends on a different continuum. Personalities who are excessively uncertain about how to cope and excessively anxious when they attempt to secure their basic needs have often been called *neurotic*. The inner emotional turmoil a neurotic personality experiences most often arises from "conflicts" between their basic instinctual drives and their qualms of conscience. As a general rule, therefore, Scott Peck's point in *The Road Less Traveled* that neurotics suffer from too much conscience is correct.[11] These individuals are too afraid to seek satisfaction of their needs because they're overly riddled with guilt or shame when they do. In contrast, *character-disordered* personalities lack self-restraint when it comes to acting upon their primal urges. They're **not bothered enough** by what they do. Again, as Peck points out, they're the kind of people who have too little conscience.[12] It is not possible to characterize every individual as simply neurotic or character disordered, but everyone falls somewhere along the continuum between mostly neurotic and mostly character disordered. Nonetheless, it's very helpful to make the distinction about whether a person is primarily neurotic vs. disturbed in character.

Freud postulated that civilization is the cause of neurosis. He noted that the principal ways people bring pain and hardship into the lives of others involve acts of sex or aggression and that society often condemns indiscriminate sexual or aggressive conduct. He theorized, therefore, that persons who internalize societal prohibitions, though transformed from savages, pay a price for their self-restraint in the form of neurosis. From another point of view, however, one could say that the willingness of most per-sons to restrain (or even worry about) their sexual and aggressive urges is what makes civilization possible. Rare is the person who "owns" and *freely* disciplines their basic instincts and, therefore, in the manner Carl Jung suggested is possible,[13] *transcends* all neurosis. For the most part, therefore, it's our capacity for neurosis that keeps us civilized. Neurosis is a very functional phenomenon then, in moderation. In today's permissive social climate, it is much less common that an individual's neurosis has become so extreme that therapeutic intervention is necessary, and moderately neurotic individuals are the backbone of our society.

In a civilized society character-disordered individuals are more problematic than neurotics. Neurotics mainly cause problems for themselves because they let their excessive and unwarranted fears stifle their own success. And this happens only in those relatively rare cases where neurosis is excessive. Contrarily, character-disordered personalities, unencumbered by qualms of conscience, passionately pursue their personal goals with indifference to—and often at the expense of—the rights and needs of others,[14] and cause all sorts of problems for others and society at large. A common saying among professionals is that if a person is making himself miserable, he's probably neurotic, and if he's making everyone else miserable, he's probably character-disordered. Among the various personality types, submissive personalities are among the most neurotic and the aggressive personalities are among the most character-disordered.

Very contrasting characteristics define mostly neurotic versus mostly character-disordered individuals. These differences are crucial to remember, whether you're a person in a problematic relationship or a therapist trying to understand and remedy an unhealthy situation.

NEUROTIC PERSONALITY

- For neurotics, anxiety plays a major role in the development of their personality and fuels their "symptoms" of distress.

- Neurotics have a well-developed, or perhaps even overactive conscience or superego.

- Neurotics have an excessive capacity for guilt and or shame. This increases anxiety and causes much of their distress.

- Neurotics employ defense mechanisms to help reduce anxiety and protect themselves from unbearable emotional pain.

- Fear of social rejection prompts neurotics to mask their true self and present a false façade to others.

- The psychological "symptoms" of distress neurotics experience are ego-dystonic (i.e. experienced as unwanted and undesirable). For this reason, neurotics often voluntarily seek help to alleviate their distress.

- Emotional conflicts underlie the symptoms reported by neurotics and are the appropriate focus of therapy.

- Neurotics often have damaged or deficient self-esteem.

- Neurotics are hypersensitive to adverse consequence and social rejection.

- Inner emotional conflicts that cause anxiety for neurotics and the defense mechanisms they use to reduce this anxiety are largely unconscious.

- Because the root of problems is often unconscious, neurotics need and often benefit from the increased self-awareness that traditional, *insight-oriented* therapy approaches offer.

DISORDERED CHARACTER

- Anxiety plays a minor role in the problems experienced by the character-disordered individual (CDO). CDOs lack sufficient apprehension and anxiety related to their dysfunctional behavior pattern.

- The extremely disordered character may have no conscience at all. Most CDOs have consciences that are significantly underdeveloped.

- CDOs have diminished capacities for experiencing genuine shame or guilt.

- What may appear a defense mechanism to some is more likely a power tactic used to manipulate others and resist making concessions to societal demands.

- CDO individuals may try to manage your impression of them, but in basic personality, they are who they are.

- Problematic aspects of personality are ego-syntonic (i.e. CDOs like who they are and are comfortable with their behavior patterns, even though who they are and how they act might bother others a lot). They rarely seek help on their own but are usually pressured by others.

- Erroneous thinking patterns/attitudes underlie the problem behaviors CDOs display.

- CDOs most often have inflated self-esteem. Their inflated self-image is not a compensation for underlying feelings of inadequacy.

- CDOs are undeterred by adverse consequence or societal condemnation.

- The CDO's problematic behavior patterns may be habitual and automatic, but they are conscious and deliberate.

- The disordered character has plenty of insight and awareness but despite it, resists changing his/her attitudes and core beliefs. CDOs don't need any more insight. What they need and can benefit from are limits, confrontation, and most especially, correction. Cognitive-behavioral therapeutic approaches are the most appropriate.

As outlined, on almost every dimension, disturbed characters are very different from neurotic individuals. Most especially, disordered characters don't think the way most of us do. In recent years, researchers have come to realize the importance of recognizing that fact. How we think, what we believe, and the attitudes we've developed largely determine how we will act. That's partly why current research indicates that cognitive-behavioral therapy (confronting erroneous thinking patterns and reinforcing a person's willingness to change their thinking and behavior patterns) is the treatment of choice for disturbed characters.

Research into the distorted thinking patterns of disordered characters began several years ago and focused on the thinking patterns of criminals. Over the years, researchers have come to understand that problematic patterns of thinking are common to all types of disordered characters, I have adopted, modified, and added to many of the known problematic patterns of thinking and offer a brief summary of some of the more important ones:

- **Self-Focused (self-centered) thinking**. Disordered characters are always thinking of themselves. They don't think about what others need or how their behavior might impact others. This kind of thinking leads to attitudes of selfishness and disregard for social obligation.

- **Possessive thinking**. This is thinking of people as possessions to do with as I please or whose role it is to please me. Disturbed characters also tend to see others as objects (objectification) as opposed to individuals with dignity, worth, rights and needs. This kind of thinking leads to attitudes of ownership, entitlement and dehumanization.

- **Extreme (all-or-none) thinking**. The disordered character tends to think that if he can't have everything he wants, he won't accept anything. If he's not on top, he sees himself at the bottom. If someone doesn't agree with everything he says, he thinks they don't value his opinions at all. This kind of thinking keeps him from any sense of balance or moderation and promotes an uncompromising attitude.

- **Egomaniacal thinking**. The disordered character so overvalues himself that he thinks that he is entitled to whatever he wants. He tends to think that things are owed him, as opposed to accepting that he needs to earn the things he desires. This kind of thinking promotes attitudes of superiority, arrogance, and entitlement.

- **Shameless thinking**. A healthy sense of shame is lacking in the disturbed character. He tends not to care how his behavior reflects on him as a character. He may be embarrassed if someone exposes his true character, but embarrassment at being uncovered is not the same as feeling shameful about reprehensible conduct. Shameless thinking fosters an attitude of brazenness.

- **Quick and easy thinking**. The disturbed character always wants things the easy way. He hates to put forth effort or accept obligation. He gets far more joy out of "conning" people. This way of thinking promotes an attitude of disdain for labor and effort.

- **Guiltless thinking**. Never thinking of the rightness or wrongness of a behavior before he acts, the disturbed character takes whatever he wants, no matter what societal norm is violated. This kind of thinking fosters an attitude of irresponsibility and anti-sociality.

Aggressive Personalities and Aggressive Personality Subtypes

The personality theorist Theodore Millon conceptualizes aggressive personalities as actively-independent[15] in the way they interact with others and deal with the world at large. He points out that these individuals actively take charge of getting their needs met and resist depending on the support of others. He also suggests that there are two kinds of actively-independent personality, one able to conform his conduct well enough to function in society, and the other unable to abide by the rule of law.[16] I do not agree that the label "aggressive" best describes the interpersonal style of every subtype of actively independent personality. A person can adopt a style of actively taking care of himself without being truly aggressive about it. Such is the case with the assertive personality, which I regard as the healthiest of all personalities. But I wholeheartedly agree that there are many more types of aggressive personalities than career criminals and it is unfortunate that the official psychiatric nomenclature only recognizes a small subtype of the active-independent personality, the *antisocial* personality, as psychologically disordered.

Unlike the assertive personality, aggressive personalities pursue their interpersonal agendas with a degree of ruthlessness that bespeaks their disregard for the rights and needs of others. Their core characteristics include a predisposition to meet life's challenges head-on and with a steadfast determination to "win," a feisty temperament and mind-set, a maladaptive lack of fearfulness and inhibitory control, a persistent desire to be in the dominant position, and a particular kind of disdain and disregard for those perceived as weaker. They are "fighters" to the core.

Aggressive personalities also share most of the characteristics of narcissists. In fact, some see this personality type as merely an aggressive variant of the narcissistic personality. Aggressive personalities are notoriously self-confident and self-absorbed. Their wants, their agendas, their plans, etc. are all that matter to them. And anyone or anything standing in their way must be rendered incapable of thwarting their goals.

Drawing from Millon's formulations about actively-independent personalities, some of the research on Type "A" (aggressive) personalities,[17] emerging research on some of the most severely aggressive personalities, and years of clinical experience working with disturbed characters of all sorts, I find it useful to categorize five basic aggressive personality types: the unbridled-aggressive, channeled-aggressive, sadistic, predatory (psychopathic) and covert-aggressive personalities. Although they have much in common with one another, each of these aggressive personality types has some clearly unique defining characteristics. Some are more dangerous than others and some are more difficult to understand than others. But all of the aggressive personalities pose considerable challenges to those who have to work for them, live with them, or labor under their influence.

Unbridled-Aggressive personalities are openly hostile, frequently violent and often criminal in their behavior. These are the people we commonly label *antisocial*. They tend to be easily angered, lack adaptive fearfulness or cautiousness, are impulsive, reckless, and risk-taking, and are overly prone to violate the rights of others. Many spend a good deal of their lives incarcerated because they simply won't conform, even when it's in their best interest. Traditional thinking on these personalities has always been that they are the way they are because they grew up in circumstances that made them mistrust authority and others and were too scarred from abuse and neglect to adequately "bond" to others. My experience over the years has convinced me that some of these overtly aggressive personalities have indeed been fueled in their hostility by an inordinate mistrust of others. An even smaller number appear to be biologically predisposed to extreme vigilance and suspiciousness (i.e., have some paranoid personality traits as well). But my experience has taught me that most unbridled aggressive personalities are not so much driven by mis-trust and suspicion, but rather an excessive readiness to aggress, even when unnecessary, unprompted, or fueled by anger. They will aggress without hesitation or regard to consequence either to themselves or others. And a fair number of these individuals do not have abuse, neglect, or disadvantage in their backgrounds. Indeed, some were the beneficiaries of the best of circumstances. So, many of our traditional assumptions about these personalities are being re-evaluated. One researcher has noted that about the only reliable common factor he could find among all of the various "criminal personalities" he had worked with was that they all seemed to enjoy engaging in illicit activity.

Channeled-Aggressives are overtly aggressive personalities who generally confine their aggression to socially acceptable outlets such as business, sports, law enforcement, the legal profession and the military. These people are often rewarded for being tough, headstrong, and competitive. They may openly talk about "burying" the competition or "crushing" their opponents. They don't usually cross the line into truly antisocial behavior but it really shouldn't surprise anyone when they do. That's because their social conformity is often more a matter of practicality rather than a true submission to a set of principles or higher authority. So, they'll break the rules and inflict undue harm on others when they feel justified in so doing, or when they think they can get away with it.

The **Sadistic Aggressive** personality is another overtly aggressive personality subtype. Like all other aggressive personalities, they seek positions of power and dominance over others. But these individuals gain particular satisfaction from seeing their victims squirm and grovel in positions of vulnerability. For the other aggressive personality types, inflicting pain or injury on anyone standing in the way of something they want are seen as merely hazards of the fight. *Most of the aggressive personalities don't set out to hurt, they set out to win.* The way they see it, if someone has to get hurt for them to have their way, then so be it. The sadist, however, *enjoys* making people grovel and suffer. Like the other aggressive personalities, sadists want to dominate and control, but they particularly enjoy doing that by humiliating and denigrating their victims.

The **Predatory Aggressive** is the most dangerous of the aggressive personalities (also referred to by some as the psychopath or sociopath). There is perhaps no more learned expert on this topic than Robert Hare, whose book *Without Conscience* is a chilling but very readable and valuable primer on the subject. Fortunately, as a group, psychopaths are relatively uncommon. However, in my career I have encountered and dealt with a fair number of them. These characters are radically different from most people. Their lack of conscience is unnerving. They tend to see themselves as superior creatures for whom the inferior, common man is rightful *prey*. They are the *most extreme manipulators* or con artists who thrive on exploiting and abusing others. They can be charming and disarming. As highly skilled predators, they study the vulnerabilities of their prey carefully and are capable of the most heinous acts of victimization with no sense of remorse or regret. Fortunately, most manipulators aren't psychopaths.

The various aggressive personalities have certain characteristics in common. They are all excessively prone to seek a position of power and dominance over others. They are all relatively uninhibited by the threat of punishment or pangs of conscience. They also tend to view things and to think in

ways that distort reality of circumstances, prevent them from accepting and exercising responsibility over their behavior, and "justify" their overly aggressive stance. Their distorted, erroneous patterns of thinking have been the subject of much recent research.[18] Because the various aggressive personality types have so much in common, it's not unusual for one subtype to possess some of the characteristics of another. So, predominantly antisocial personalities may have some sadistic as well as covert-aggressive features and covert-aggressives may have some antisocial tendencies, etc.

As mentioned earlier, all of the aggressive personalities have many characteristics in common with narcissistic personalities. Both display ego-inflation and attitudes of entitlement. Both are exploitive in their interpersonal relationships. Both are emotion-ally independent personalities. That is, they rely on themselves to get what they need. Millon describes narcissists as passive-independent personalities[19] because they think so much of themselves that they believe that they just don't need anybody else to get along in life. They don't necessarily have to *do* anything to demonstrate their competence and superiority. They're already convinced of it. And while narcissists are so self-centered and absorbed that they might passively disregard

the rights and needs of others, the aggressive personalities, by contrast, actively engage in behaviors designed to secure and maintain their independence and actively trample upon the rights of others to secure their goals and maintain a position of dominance over others.

The Covert-Aggressive Personality

As an aggressive personality subtype, one might expect

covert-aggressives to share some of characteristics of narcissists as well as the other aggressive personalities. But covert-aggressives have many unique attributes that make them a truly distinct type of aggressive personality. These personalities are mostly distinguished from the other aggressive personality types by the way that they fight. They fight for what they want and seek power over others in subtle, cunning and underhanded ways. On balance, they are much more character disordered than neurotic. To the degree they might have some neurosis, they deceive themselves about their true character and their covertly-aggressive conduct. To the degree they are character disordered, the more they actively attempt to deceive only their intended victims.

The covert-aggressive's dislike of appearing overtly aggressive is as practical as it is face-saving. Manipulators know that if they're above-board in their aggression, they'll encounter resistance. Having learned that one of the best ways to "overcome" an obstacle is to "go around" it, they're adept at fighting unscrupulously yet surreptitiously.

Some personality theorists have proposed that the cardinal quality of the covert-aggressive or manipulative personality is that they derive an inordinate sense of exhilaration from pulling the wool over the eyes of their victims.[20] But I believe their main agenda is the same as that of the other aggressive personalities. They just want to win and have found covert ways of fighting to be the most effective way to meet their objective. I have found these to be their major attributes:

1. Covert-aggressives always want to have their way or to "win." For them, as with all aggressive personalities, every life situation is a challenge to be met, a battle to be won.

2. Covert-aggressives seek power and dominance over others. They always want to be one-up and in control. They use an arsenal of subtle but effective power tactics to gain and keep the advantage in their interpersonal relations. They use certain tactics that make it more likely that others will go on the defensive, retreat, or concede while simultaneously concealing their aggressive intent.

3. Covert-aggressives can be deceptively civil, charming and seductive. They know how to "look good' and how to win you over by "melting" your resistance. They know what to say and do to get you to abandon any intuitive mistrust and give them what they want.

4. Covert-aggressives can also be unscrupulous, underhanded, and vindictive fighters. They know how to capitalize on any weakness and will intensify their aggression if they notice you faltering. They know how to catch you unaware and unprepared. And if they think you've thwarted or gotten the better of them, they'll try to get you back. For them, the battle is never over until they think they've won.

5. Covert-aggressives have uniquely impaired consciences. Like all aggressive personalities, they lack internal "brakes." They know right from wrong, but won't let that stand in the way of getting what they want. To them, the ends *always* justify the means. So, they deceive themselves and others about what they're really doing.

6. Covert-aggressives are abusive and exploitive in their interpersonal relations. They view people as pawns in the game (contest) of life. Detesting weakness, they take advantage of every frailty they find in their "opponents."

As is the case with any other type of personality, covert-aggressives vary in their degree of psychopathology. The most seriously disturbed covert-aggressives go far beyond just being manipulative in their interpersonal style. Severely disturbed covert-aggressives are capable of masking a considerable degree of ruthlessness and power-thirstiness under a deceptively civil and even alluring social façade. Some may even be psychopathic. Jim Jones and David Koresh are good examples. But even though a covert-aggressive personality can be a lot more than just a manipulator, habitual manipulators are most always covert-aggressive personalities.

Distinguishing Covert-Aggressives From
Passive-Aggressive and Other Personality Types

Just as passive and covert-aggression are very different behaviors, passive-aggressive and covert-aggressive personalities are very different from one another. Millon describes the passive-aggressive or "negativistic" personality as one who is actively ambivalent about whether to adopt a primarily independent or dependent style of coping.[21] These individuals want to take charge of their own life, but fear they lack the capability to do so effectively. Their ambivalence about whether to primarily fend for themselves or lean on others puts them and those in relationships with them in a real bind. They chronically crave and solicit support and nurturance from others. But because they also resent being in positions of dependence and submission, they often try to gain some sense of personal power by resisting cooperation with the very people from whom they solicit support. Waffling on a decision, they might complain that you decide. When you do, they hesitate to go along. In an argument with you, they may get fed up and want to disengage. But afraid that if they truly disengage they might be emotionally abandoned, they'll stay and "pout" until you plead with them to tell you what's wrong. Life with passive-aggressive personalities can be very difficult because there often seems to be no way to please them. Although he frequently fails to distinguish passive from covert-aggression, Scott Wetzler characterizes the passive-aggressive personality and what life is like with such individuals quite well in his book *Living with the Passive-Aggressive Man.*[22]

Passive-aggressive patients in therapy are legend. They may "whine" and complain about the lack of support they're getting from the therapist. But as soon as the therapist tries to give them something, they inevitably start "bucking" the therapist's suggestions with "yes..., but" statements and other subtle forms of passive-resistance. Most therapists can readily distinguish these actively "ambivalent" personalities who are driven by a hypersensitivity to shame from the more cunning, calculating manipulators I call covert-aggressive. But sometimes, unfamiliar with the more accurate term, and wanting to highlight the subtle aggression manipulators display, therapists often misuse the label "passive-aggressive" to describe manipulators. Covert-aggressive personalities are not the same as obsessive-compulsive personalities. We all know perfectionistic, meticulous and highly organized people. When they are reviewing our tax returns or performing brain surgery, we value these attributes quite highly. Yes, *some* compulsive people can be forceful, authoritarian, domineering and controlling. But that's because these kinds of people are also covertly aggressive. A person can use their purported commitment to principles and standards as a vehicle for wielding power and dominance over others. Obsessive-compulsive people who are also covertly aggressive are the kind of people who attempt to shove their own standards down everyone else's throats.

Covert-aggressive personalities are not identical to narcissistic personalities, although they almost always have narcissistic characteristics. People who think too much of themselves don't necessarily attempt to manipulate others. Narcissists can passively disregard the needs of others because of how absorbed they are with themselves. Some self-centered people, however, actively disregard the needs others and intentionally victimize and abuse them. Recognizing this, some writers have distinguished the benign from the malignant narcissist. But I think the difference between the kind of person who is too self-absorbed to be inattentive to the rights and needs of others and the kind of person who habitually exploits and victimizes is that the latter, in addition to being narcissistic, is distinctly aggressive. So, egotists who cleverly exploit and manipulate others are not just narcissistic, they're also covertly aggressive personalities.

Most covert-aggressive personalities are not antisocial. Because they have a disregard for the rights and needs of others, have very impaired consciences, actively strive to gain advantage over others, and try to get away with just about anything short of blatant crime or overt aggression, it's tempting to label them antisocial. Indeed, some antisocial individuals use manipulation as part of their overall modus operandi. However, manipulators don't violate major social norms, lead lives of crime, or violently aggress against others, although they are capable of these things. Several attempts have been made to accurately describe the calculating, underhanded, controlling interpersonal style of manipulative people. They've been called all sorts of things from sociopathic to malignantly narcissistic, and even, as Scott Peck suggests, "evil."[23] Sensing the subtly aggressive character of their behavior, many have called them passive-aggressive. But none of these labels accurately defines the core characteristic of manipulative personalities. It's important to recognize that for the most part, manipulation involves covert-aggression and habitual manipulators are covert-aggressive personalities.

It's also important to remember that a manipulative person

may have other personality characteristics in addition to their covert-aggressive propensities. So, in addition to being manipulative, they may have narcissistic, obsessive-compulsive, antisocial or other tendencies. But as a friend of mine once remarked, "It may have short ears and it may have long ears; it may have a lot of hair and it may have no hair at all; it may be brown or it may be gray; but if it's big and has tusks and a trunk, it's always an elephant." As long as the person you're dealing with possesses the core attributes outlined earlier, no matter what else they are, they're a covert-aggressive personality.

Because the predatory aggressive or psychopathic personality is so adept at manipulation, some might tend to view the covert-aggressive personality as a milder variant of the psychopath. This is a fair perspective. Psychopaths are the most dangerous, cunning, and manipulative of the aggressive personalities. Fortunately, however, they are also the most uncommon. The manipulative personalities described in this book are much more common and, although they can wreak a good deal of havoc in the lives of their victims, they are not as dangerous as psychopaths.

How Someone Becomes a Covert-Aggressive Personality

How any aggressive personality gets to be the way they are varies. I have seen individuals whose early lives were so full of abuse and neglect that they had to become strong "fighters" just to survive. I've also met plenty of individuals who seemed to have fought too much all of their lives despite growing up in the most nurturing and supportive environments. These persons seem to have "bucked" the process of socialization from early on and their character development appears to have been heavily influenced at every stage by their excessive combativeness. But regardless of whether nature or nurture is the stronger influence, somehow in their childhood development, most covert-aggressive personalities seem to have over-learned some, and failed to learn other essential lessons about managing their aggression. Judging from the histories with which I am familiar, covertly aggressive personalities typically exhibit the following learning failures:

1. They never learned when fighting is really necessary and just. To them, daily living is a battle and anything that stands in the way of something they want is the "enemy." Obsessed with "winning," they're far too willing and too ready to fight.

2. They never allowed themselves to learn that "winning" in the long-run is often characterized by a willingness to give ground, concede, or submit in the short-run. They failed to recognize those times when it's best to acquiesce. Their total aversion to submission prevents them from making the little concessions in life that often lead to "victory" later on.

3. They never learned how to fight constructively or fairly. They might have learned to mistrust their ability to win a fair fight. Perhaps they were never willing to run the risk of losing. Sometimes, it's just because they found covert fighting to be so effective. Whatever the case, somehow they over-learned how to "win" (at least, in the short-run) by fighting underhandedly and surreptitiously.

4. Because they detest submission, they never allowed themselves to learn the potentially constructive benefits of admitting defeat. I think this dynamic is at the heart of the apparent failure of all aggressive (and character-disordered) personalities to learn what we want them to learn from past experience. Truly learning (i.e. internalizing) a lesson in life always involves submitting oneself to a higher authority, power, or moral principle. The reason aggressive personalities don't change is because they don't submit.

5. They never learned to get beyond their childish selfishness and self-centeredness. They failed to realize that they're not necessarily entitled to go after something just because they want it. To them, the entire world is their oyster. Having become skilled at getting their way through manipulation, they come to think of themselves as invincible. This further inflates their already grandiose self-image.

6. They never learned genuine respect or empathy for the vulnerabilities of others. To them, everyone else's weakness is simply their advantage. Having only disdain for weakness, especially emotional weakness, they over-learned how to find and push their victims' emotional "buttons."

Fertile Ground for Covert-Aggression

Some professions, social institutions and fields of endeavor provide great opportunities for covert-aggressive personalities to exploit others. Politics, law enforcement and religion are some prime examples. I am not implying that all politicians, law enforcement professionals or religious leaders are manipulative personalities. However, covert power-seekers that they are, manipulators cannot help but gravitate toward and exploit the excellent opportunities for self-advancement and the wielding of considerable power under the guise of service available in such endeavors. The televangelists, cult leaders, political extremists, Sunday night TV "success" peddlers and militant social activists who have been exposed in the headlines lately are no different in their over-all modus operandi from the covert-aggressives we encounter in everyday life. They're just more extreme cases. The more cunning and skilled at using the tactics of manipulation a covert-aggressive is, the easier it is for them to rise to a position of substantial power and influence.

Understanding and Dealing With Manipulative People

It's easy to fall victim to the covert-aggressive's ploys. Anyone wanting to avoid victimization will need to:

1. Get intimately acquainted with the character of these wolves in sheep's clothing. Get to know what they really want and how they operate. Know them so intimately that you can always spot one when you encounter one. The stories in the following chapters are written in a genre that will hopefully make it easier for you to get the "flavor" of the covert-aggressive personality.

2. Become acquainted with the favorite tactics covertly aggressive people use to manipulate and control others. We not only need to know what covert-aggressives are like, but also what kinds of behaviors we should expect from them. In general, we can expect them to do whatever it takes to "win," but knowing their most common "tactics" well and recognizing when they are being used is most helpful in avoiding victimization.

3. Become aware of the fears and insecurities most of us possess that increase our vulnerability to the covert-aggressive's ploys. Knowing your own weaknesses can be your foremost strength in dealing more effectively with a manipulator.

4. Learn what changes you can make in your own behavior to reduce your vulnerability to victimization and exploitation. Using techniques such those presented in Chapter 10 can radically change the nature of your interactions with others and empower you to deal more effectively with those who would otherwise manipulate and control you.

The stories in the next few chapters are designed to help you become more intimately acquainted with the character of manipulative people. Each chapter highlights one of the distinguishing characteristics of covertly aggressive personalities. In each story, I'll attempt to highlight the manipulators' main agendas, what power tactics they employ to advance them, and the weaknesses they exploit in their victims.

THE DETERMINATION TO WIN

The primary characteristic of covert-aggressive personalities is that they value winning over everything. Determined, cunning and sometimes ruthless, they use a variety of manipulative tactics, not only to get what they want, but also to avoid seeing themselves or being seen by others as the kind of people they really are. The story of Joe and Mary Blake will give you an idea of how much pain can enter the lives of members of a family in which one person, under the guise of care and concern, is too determined to have his way.

The Father Who Wanted A's

Lisa Blake was having nightmares again. She was increasingly irritable and occasionally uncooperative. Her performance in school was deteriorating. Her parents, Joe and Mary, knew that such behavior is relatively common in preadolescence. But it was very unusual for Lisa. Lisa was their one and only child. They were quite concerned.

Joe had devoted much of his time and energy toward figuring out what to do about Lisa. Mary had suggested several times that Lisa might just be under a lot of pressure.

But Joe was certain the problem was more than that, and he

had made every effort to have Mary see his point of view. He stressed how deeply he cared about his daughter's welfare. He kept saying he believed any really good parent would leave no stone unturned until a solution was found.

Joe had already done so much in his effort to help Lisa. When she brought home the first B's on her report card a few months ago, he expressed concern to the school officials that she might have some learning disabilities. But the teachers balked at the notion of testing Lisa again. They told him that she was doing just fine. Joe let them know that he cared too much about his daughter's welfare not to rule out the possibility. For some time, he had suspected the resource room teacher was simply not very eager to have another child in the special classroom. Mary expressed doubt about the advisability of a move, but Joe made her see they had no choice but to remove Lisa from a school with so little apparent teacher dedication and enroll her in a private school where parental concern and involvement would be more appreciated.

After remaining on the honor roll for the first semester at her new school, Lisa's grades began to slip again. In addition, she was starting to be more disobedient over little things, and especially with Joe. Joe knew something had to be done. He scheduled a complete academic and psychological evaluation for Lisa at a reputable clinic. He was a little surprised the people he talked to there wanted to interview the whole family in addition to testing Lisa. But, as he'd said many times, he was prepared to do anything to help his daughter.

Mary felt reassured by the counselor's feedback. She was also encouraged by Lisa's comments on the way home from the clinic. "The lady there told me I could come to see her any time to talk about things," Lisa said, "I think I'd like that." Joe, however, was pretty aggravated about some of the things the counselor said. "Imagine!" he exclaimed as he made the case to Mary that the counselor was wrong and he was right, "They tried to tell me that *my* Lisa has *average* intelligence! She used to get all A's and always made the honor roll!" Does that seem like *average* intelligence?" Joe also had some thoughts about the counselor's suggestions that Lisa was pushing herself too hard and that some nightmares she'd been having suggested she had some anger toward her parents, especially her father, for expecting too much of her. Eventually he convinced Mary that those psychologically-minded folks at the clinic probably "meant well," but they didn't know his daughter—at least, not like he did.

Joe was grinning from ear-to-ear when he announced his surprise the next day. He'd found a solution to Lisa's problem. He revealed that he'd purchased a new computer and several top-notch tutorial programs. Now, he and Lisa could spend a couple of hours together each day working on practice exercises that would get her "back on track." He could pay for the cost of it with the money he saved by not sending Lisa to the clinic anymore. If Lisa were mad at him for any reason, like the counselors suggested, working so closely together each day should solve that problem. Best of all, he knew he could get back the same little girl he'd always known. After all, he told himself, nobody could care for his little girl like her daddy could.

When a Person Stops at Nothing

Joe told Mary several times that he wanted only the best for his daughter. He lied. Not only did he lie to Mary, he lied to himself. He may have had himself convinced and he certainly did his best to convince others that he was fervently seeking his daughter's welfare. In reality, however, he just wanted Lisa to bring home A's.

I know Joe. He's always determined to have what he wants. He always thinks he's right—that his way is the correct way—the only way. This attitude has taken him far in the business world. Some people call him a perfectionist. Others say he's demanding, obsessive and controlling. But these labels don't fully capture what's unhealthy about him. The bottom line is that Joe always wants his way and doesn't know when to stop—when to concede—when to back off. He's the kind of guy who'll stop at nothing to get what he wants. Sometimes, that's good. To be a "winner" in life, a little such determination is necessary. But when Joe is aggressing at the wrong time and in the wrong arena, and especially *when he purports to be doing anything but aggressing,* his behavior can be extremely destructive.

Joe is also vain. He sees his family as a reflection of himself. In his mind, it's Lisa's duty to present a favorable image to others so that others will be impressed with him. Joe is wrapped-up in himself and his social image. Despite protestations to the contrary, he is insensitive to the wants and needs of others. As self-absorbed as he is, it's not possible for him to have much empathy for his daughter. But Joe's vanity isn't the direct cause of Lisa's and Mary's pain. His readiness to shove his will down everyone else's throats, always under the guise of care and concern (his covert-aggression), is the major cause of problems.

This case exemplifies how some individuals, despite surface-level appearances, can wield significant emotional tyranny in their homes. It is based on a real clinical case. You might find it interesting that Lisa's nightmares had a common theme. Her dreams were mostly about someone wanting to hurt her father. Classical analysis would suggest that Lisa probably had some unconscious desires to hurt, or even kill her father. Lisa intuitively sensed Joe's ruthlessness but she is not the type to lash out. So, she only felt safe enough to express her feelings in her dreams.

How Joe Manipulates Mary

Now, the question arises about how Mary seems to get manipulated into seeing things Joe's way, when in her heart she thinks he's being unreasonable. So, there are some other facts about this case that we need to explore. The fact is that Joe is expert at using some very effective tactics to quash any resistance Mary might think to offer.

Joe knows that Mary is extremely conscientious. He knows that if she thinks that she's in any way neglecting a duty or falling short of her responsibilities as a wife and mother, she'll stop dead in her tracks. So when she confronts him, all he has to do is to make her believe that challenging him is tantamount to neglecting her daughter's welfare. If he can make himself appear as the one who really cares, then Mary might be tempted to believe she's the callous one.

In the preceding vignette, Joe used some very effective tactics (which will be explored in more detail in Chapter 9) to convince himself that he was justified in what he was doing and to convince Mary that she'd be wrong to resist him. He *rationalized* his selfish agenda both to himself and to his family. His rationalizations promoted the notion that no one else shared the level of interest in his daughter that he did. He pointed out all the times the teachers at Lisa's old school "dropped the ball" or "sloughed-off" a problem. As is the case with rationalizations, they made just enough sense to Mary that she became convinced if she didn't go along with Joe, it would mean she didn't care as much as he did about Lisa. Joe's rationalizations masked his true agenda. What he wanted was a super-achieving daughter who would serve as a positive reflection on him and further feed his already substantial ego. It wasn't his daughter's welfare about which he cared. It was his hunger for self-aggrandizement that he wanted to satisfy.

Joe also engaged in substantial *denial* about his role in any of his daughter's difficulties and *projected the blame* onto others. If he for one minute allowed himself to view himself as a culprit, he might have had second thoughts. His denial is not just the way he protects or "defends" his self-image as classical psychology theories postulate, it's the vehicle by which he grants himself per-mission to keep on doing what he might otherwise not do. This is so important to recognize. At the time he engages in denial, Joe is not primarily protecting or defending anything. He's mainly *fighting* to overcome all obstacles in the way of getting what he wants and resisting any submission to the will of others.

Joe knows how to keep Lisa under his thumb, too. He gives subtle, constant (albeit nonverbal) messages to her that if she does just as he expects, they will be close and she will be his "little girl." But if she bucks him, tries to assert herself, or fails to live up to expectations, he slyly lets her know there will be some sort of hell to pay.

I remember how subtle but effective Joe could be with his *implied (veiled) threats* to punish anyone who wasn't going along with him. At times, just the looks he would give could be quite intimidating. Even the trip to the clinic for "evaluation" and "nipping this willful defiance thing in the bud" was used as a carefully veiled but nonetheless threatened punishment.

As a seasoned power broker, Joe is very aware of anything that might upset the balance of power in his family. When the treatment team at the clinic made the whole idea of counseling palatable to Lisa, and she saw it as an opportunity to vent her feelings as opposed to a punishment, Joe quickly took the opportunity away. He graciously informed the treatment team that everything was worked out and our services would no longer be needed. He knew the balance of power might be disrupted. He did what he needed to do to maintain power, control and a position of dominance.

Lisa's case was an instructive treatment failure. From it, I learned that if you're going to try and help anyone else in a manipulator's family win, you can't just let the manipulator feel like they have to lose. The importance of crafting win-win scenarios in dealings with manipulators will be discussed in more detail in Chapter 10.

THE UNBRIDLED QUEST FOR POWER

Nothing is more important to any aggressive personality than gaining power and achieving a position of dominance over others. In real estate, there is the old adage that three things are important: location, location, and location. For any aggressive personality, only three things matter: position, position, and position! Now, we all want some sense of power in our lives. That's not unhealthy. But how ambitiously we pursue it, how we go about preserving it, and how we use it when we have it says a lot about the kind of person we are. Covert-aggressives are ruthlessly ambitious people but they're careful not to be perceived that way. The following story is about a man of the cloth who lies to himself and his family about the real master he serves.

The Minister on a Mission

James was just a little hesitant the day he, Jean, and the children left their cozy cottage next to the historic, countryside church. He'd already told the children how the move to the city would bring excitement and opportunity for them. They'd have so much more to do, and they wouldn't complain as much that he never seemed to find the time to go camping or river rafting with them. He quelled the uneasiness Jean shared with him about the added stress serving a larger congregation might bring to their relationship. He was very convincing as he pointed out to her how she'd always had a hard time accepting that the Lord's work comes first. Jean acknowledged her "selfishness" and renewed her pledge that James would have her support.

The small congregation was buzzing for weeks about the move. Rumor had it that the Capital City congregation had always been the grooming grounds for future Church Elders. James responded to questions with his customary humility: "I don't know what the Master has in store for me..., I just go where He leads me."

The pastor of the Capital City congregation was struck by James' apparent dedication and fervor. He reminded him on several occasions it wasn't necessary to answer every request for a home visit or drop in on almost every Bible study meeting. But James said that he found serving the Lord "energizing" and tended his flock with great vigor.

The crowd that would gather following Sunday services seemed to be getting larger with each impassioned sermon. James appeared to blush at the frequent praise from parishioners extolling his dedication. He responded that ministering to the needs of others brought him untold joy and contentment. He told everyone how happy he was just to be the Lord's humble servant.

Everyone seemed to love and revere James. That's what made it so difficult for Jean to talk to him again. She still felt some-what guilty and, as James had suggested to her more than once, a little selfish. But she was becoming weary of the lonely nights.

She wanted time to talk things over and to have his assistance in helping the kids with their adjustment to a new school and new neighborhood. She even asked him to take back the still vacant position at the old country mission. James was adamant about staying. In an impetuous moment Jean threatened to leave. But by the time she and James finished discussing matters, she felt ever so guilty. He was right, she thought, to point out how insignificant the desires of individuals are when compared to the will of God. "If it weren't God's will, why did this opportunity come along?" he countered. Jean resigned herself to just keep trying. She did her best to help her children understand as well.

James was a little taken back with what the pastor had to say at their weekly conference. "You know, James, some people are already talking about you enrolling in training for a seat on the Elder's Council and I couldn't agree more." He continued, "I can't imagine why anyone would suggest you might be having some problems at home that might interfere with things. If I thought there were any truth to some of the rumors, I wouldn't be recommending you."

That night Jean could not believe her ears. The babysitter was all arranged. They were going out! Over dinner, James told Jean of his plans to take the whole family on a camping and fishing trip over the upcoming long weekend. He'd already worked out the details with the pastor. "What ever possessed you?" Jane inquired. "I've started to rethink some things," he replied. "And after all, you know I love you, more than life itself."

James' Hidden Agenda

James is a covert-aggressive personality. He uses the "cover" of serving the Lord and ministering to the needs of others to satisfy his ambition for prestige, position and power. His character is deeply flawed. A person of sound character has learned to balance self-interest with the interests and needs of others. James has learned no such thing. Despite claiming to be "ministering" to the needs of all the faithful, he habitually neglected the needs of his own family. Serving the needs of others is really the furthest thing from his mind. Serving his own ambition is James' true agenda. The proof of this is in James' response to his pastor's hint that a seat on the Elder's Council might be in jeopardy if there were problems at home. James instantly found time for Jean. He didn't do so because he'd had a miraculous conversion and was now the kind of person who would be more attentive to the needs of others. His thirst for power was still the agenda, though he realized that if he didn't give the appearance of a healthy home life, he would not get what he wanted.

How James Manipulates Jean

Jean is one of the most selfless, giving people I know. Perhaps she's a bit too selfless. Her unselfish devotion is James' ticket to manipulate and exploit her. When she confronts him about the need to be more attentive to his family, he uses *guilt-tripping* and subtle *shaming* tactics to invite her to believe she's asking too much. Jean is from a dysfunctional family in which toxic shame and guilt abounded. So, it's easy for her to accept invitations from others to feel ashamed or guilty.

James knows how to *play the servant role* better than most covert-aggressives I've encountered. It's hard for Jean to reconcile her gut feeling that he's being selfish and neglectful when many of his overt actions suggest he is so selflessly devoted to the ministry. Jean herself believes deeply in selfless devotion to duty. So, when James portrays himself as the servant, and casts Jean as the selfish and demanding one, Jean acquiesces.

Now the truest test of James' character (indeed, anyone's character) is how he pursues and uses power. James not only lusts for power to the detriment of his family but he abuses the power he's acquired as the Lord's spokesperson to quell the resistance he gets from his spouse. Although it's often said that power corrupts, James is living proof that power itself doesn't have the ability to corrupt a person's character. It's the already present flaw in James' character that leads him to unscrupulously pursue power in the first place and abuse it once he has it. It's the same character flaw that has led to the demise of several prominent TV evangelists in recent years. Power did not corrupt these people. It may have helped to make a bad situation worse. But these individuals' unbridled pursuit and unscrupulous use of power are the hallmarks of their already severely disturbed characters. They were power-hungry manipulators from the start.

In support of my argument that power itself does not corrupt, I offer the following. Consider the incredible degree of power a parent has over an infant child. For the crucial early years, parents literally hold the power of life or death over their children. Yet, with gratefully few exceptions, most parents wield this power with an incredible degree of trepidation and cautiousness. That's because parents of sound character are typically so conscientious about the overwhelming responsibility that's been entrusted to them, and are so committed to fulfilling that responsibility, they're not likely to abuse the power they hold. If merely having power were in itself corrupting, none of our children would have a chance.

Now, it just so happens that more and more of James' true character came to the fore as he gradually acquired power. Before long, little scrapes with certain influential members of the congregation became increasingly frequent. The run-ins he had were always about the same thing—power! The majority would want to do something one way, and James would want to do things another way. For a while, he was successful using his preferred tactics of guilt-tripping, subtle shaming and rationalization as means of getting his way. But the number of power struggles kept growing. Eventually, a group of concerned members of the congregation quietly petitioned for James' reassignment. Jean finally got her wish. James was given back his former job. Sometimes the Lord does work in mysterious ways!

chapter 4

THE PENCHANT FOR DECEPTION AND SEDUCTION

Dealing with covert-aggressive personalities is like getting whiplash. Often, you don't really know what's hit you until long after the damage is done. If you've been involved in some way with one of these smooth operators, you know how charming and disarming they can be. They are the masters of deception and seduction. They'll show you what you want to see and tell you what you want to hear. The following story is an example of a man who knows well how to charm and beguile anyone while retaining the capacity to cut out their heart.

The Story of Don and Al

Everybody liked Al. Since he'd appeared on the scene, sales were steadily increasing. Public relations were improving. What's more, morale had never been higher. Al was always so ready to compliment you and to make you feel needed. You got a feeling he really liked and appreciated you. You wanted to be on his team because you felt like he was on yours. He had that certain something—that charisma. Yes, everybody liked him.

Don wasn't sure at first. After many years in the business and working for all kinds of bosses, he'd become a little calloused.

He sometimes felt uncomfortable around Al, even when Al paid him compliments or made those frequent offers of support. But he couldn't pinpoint why he felt uncomfortable. Besides, he couldn't deny how much Al had done for the company or how much loyalty he had inspired among the employees. He also couldn't deny how refreshing it was to feel as valued and supported as Al could make you feel. So, Don grew to like him, just like everyone else.

Don wasn't sure what to make of the rumor he heard one day that Al was planning to bring in a new person. He knew he was getting older and that he wasn't setting new sales records. But Al hadn't said anything to him except for his customary compliments. In fact, he'd just given him a certificate of commendation for his years of outstanding service. He decided that the best approach would be to ask Al if he was about to be fired. "I'm glad you came to see me, Don. I'd sure hate for you to think that I wouldn't speak to you myself if I were in any way dissatisfied with you. That's the way I operate. I can assure you that you'll be able to keep your job just as long as you want it." Don felt reassured. He also felt fairly ashamed and guilty for his prior suspicions and mistrust.

The day the new man started in the same department, Don didn't know what to believe. Although Jeff admitted he'd been recruited by Al, and although Al assigned him to work in the same area, Don wasn't sure about what Jeff's role would be. All he knew was that they would both be working on commission and that if Jeff were to be assigned half of his present accounts, as Jeff said Al promised him, it would put him in a big financial bind for some time to come.

Don was mad at Al. Worst of all, he was mad about things difficult to pinpoint. He wasn't really sure if the rumor was true that Al and Jeff had known each other for quite some time and had been discussing the job for months. Nor could he be sure that the deal was struck the same day that Al personally reassured him and awarded him that certificate of appreciation. Besides, he could find no evidence that Al had clearly lied to him. It was what Al didn't say that bothered him the most. He didn't tell him that he'd soon be asked to split his client pool with a new person "for the good of the company and its future," as he explained to him later. Nor did Al indicate that he expected him, even at his age, to do his "usually fine job" of soliciting several new accounts in order to rebuild his client base. What made Don really mad, however, were Al's words of encouragement. "I still have a lot of confidence in your ability and wouldn't think of letting you go, just as I have told you before. I hope you can see your way to stay on, although I'll certainly understand if you feel you just have to go."

Don was faced with a difficult choice. He could stay on and start from scratch at a time of less than optimal health and stamina or he could take early retirement and try to make ends meet. He knew he wouldn't be able to make it on half of his usual commission. He also was becoming more certain that he'd been exploited. He began to believe Al didn't tell him anything so he wouldn't quit prematurely, upsetting the status of his accounts and potentially losing some of them. That might have cost the company money and tarnished Al's image as one of the company's "rising stars." What made matters worse for Don is how alone he felt. A lot of people still liked Al.

A Smooth Operator

We all know somebody just like Al. Undoubtedly clever and charming, he seduces others into giving him loyalty by appearing to support them. In truth, Al's only real interest is self-advancement. Al also lies. Maybe he doesn't lie overtly, but he lies by omission (covertly) with ease. He wasn't being *completely* honest when Don asked him about his future with the company. True, he didn't have any plans to fire him, and was prepared to keep him on if he had to, but he did hope to "put the squeeze" on Don and hoped he'd eventually leave of his own accord. By refraining from overt lying, he preserved apparent integrity. *Lying by omission*, he more effectively carried out his dirty work.

Don will eventually be too big a burden on his company. Al could have been direct with him about that. But he wasn't direct, instead he *evaded* the issue. This was not out of concern for Don's feelings but purely for personal advantage. The new man would need time to establish himself and Don could be invaluable in helping him learn the ropes. A negative reaction from Don's accounts if he quit or was fired might tarnish Al's glowing image. Plus, if Don resigns, while still being assured a job, Al can still preserve his image as a good guy. Such slick maneuvering is the hallmark of a covert-aggressive personality.

"Don" was never my patient, but I am intimately acquainted with his ordeal with Al. It just so happens that "Al" would later show himself for the character he truly is. He committed a heinous crime for which he is presently serving time in prison. As successful as he'd been pulling the wool over everyone's eyes for so long, he actually thought he'd get away with it. Fortunately, he didn't. But this story should give you an idea of the serious flaws in his character that were present long before fate revealed the ruthlessness he had successfully cloaked for a long time.

FIGHTING DIRTY

Some say that it's dog-eat-dog in the business world and one has to claw one's way to the top. But there's a difference between the fair competition that breeds excellence and the crafty, under-handed maneuvering that sometimes wreaks havoc in the workplace. Having to work with a covertly aggressive co-worker can be a significant source of occupational stress.

The following is the story of a woman who never fights openly or fairly for what she wants. Neither her drive, ambition, nor her desire for power and position are problems in themselves. Properly managed, these are desirable traits in anyone trying to get ahead in their organization and help their co-workers achieve excellence. The really disturbing thing about her is the devious way she goes about getting what she wants.

The Most Dedicated Woman in the Company

For a woman without prior training or experience in an executive position, everyone agreed that Betty was, nonetheless, one of the key people in the firm. Whenever the boss needed a special task accomplished, he could count on Betty's willingness to work hard and get the job done. She was familiar with most operations within the organization, having survived several changes in administration. She was indispensable.

Despite her value to almost every department, not everyone felt comfortable around Betty. There was an uneasy feeling that one could experience whenever disagreeing with her. One of her co-workers once remarked that the one time he challenged Betty, he got a feeling in his gut like the time he came close to his neighbor's fence and the Doberman Pinscher on the other side growled and bared its teeth. No one could point to anything specific that Betty had done overtly cruel to anyone. But almost intuitively, everyone knew it would be unwise to make an enemy of her.

When Jack came on board as the new executive assistant, many in the organization had high hopes for some positive changes. Betty let the boss know that despite the fact that several others had failed in the role, she would do her best to help Jack "learn the ropes." The boss expressed his usual gratitude for her willingness to be of service. He introduced Jack to Betty, letting him know that she could be his greatest resource and advising him to treat her well.

Betty seemed so helpful to Jack. She was frequently complimentary of him too, even though she knew many of the changes he wanted to make wouldn't work. She always made a point to tell the boss that she believed Jack had the best of intentions even if his ideas were "underdeveloped." She even made it a point to tell her co-workers to "just give Jack time" to learn and to mellow and then they wouldn't have to worry about some of the things he was trying to do. In the meantime, she assured everyone she would keep her usual watchful eye on things and be sure to keep the boss "informed" in her regular visits with him.

It was a bit of a surprise to Betty that some of her co-workers actually seemed to like some of the changes Jack was making. It was a bigger surprise, however, when the boss began to change the nature of some of his comments to her in their weekly meetings. He less frequently told her things like: "I'm glad you're keeping an eye on things." On the contrary, she began to hear things like: "I wasn't sure about Jack's idea at first but now it's beginning to make some sense" and "It seems as though the workers are behind Jack's new program—maybe we've found the right person for the job." Perhaps, however, her biggest surprise was discovering she had less and less to do.

People were growing increasingly fond of Jack and Betty knew it. One day, while having lunch with the boss's wife, she was surprised to learn just how personally attached to Jack her employer was becoming. She also learned some things about her boss that she didn't know before. She found out how quirky and closed-minded he could be, like the time he fired a chauffeur after learning he was gay.

Betty would later tell a friend how much it pained her to approach her boss when she did. After all, she said, she didn't really want to hurt Jack. She just thought her boss would be better informed and the company better served if the whole truth about Jack were known. "I just want you to know that it's the short-sighted plans he's making that I disagree with sir. You know, I personally like Jack," she insisted. "I know some of the others talk about it, but whatever his sexual orientation is doesn't bother me at all." Jack was becoming increasingly distressed about the growing distance between himself and the boss. He couldn't imagine why the rapport they'd established had so rapidly deteriorated. Due to decreased access to his supervisor, he became increasingly reliant upon Betty to provide him with information as well as to advocate his plans. She helped him see that the boss was becoming increasingly dissatisfied with some of his work but didn't want to undergo the emotional ordeal that it would be to fire him. He was even somewhat comforted by the fact that Betty went to the trouble of giving him some leads about possible openings at another firm.

Everyone was surprised the day that Jack left. Everyone, that is, except Betty. She's told herself several times and tried to tell the others that he just wasn't the right person for the job. After all, she'd been there long enough to know what's best for the company. But she couldn't spend time worrying about Jack, or anyone else who might attempt to take his place. She had lots of work to do.

Dirty Dealing

I am well aware of the stereotyping people do in the workplace about the office "bitch" and the sexism inherent in this most of the time. I'm also aware of the double standard often applied when it comes to making value judgments about men and women who exhibit any kind of aggressive behavior. So, I know that examining Betty's aggressive character is fraught with potentially politically incorrect danger. But I don't really think the uncomfortable feeling you probably had when reading about Betty is just because she is a woman who is being aggressive. It's the *way* Betty does what she does that gets to you. It's her dirty, underhanded way of fighting.

What You Don't Know Can Hurt You

Jack got manipulated out of a job largely because he was naïve about territoriality in the competitive workplace and how aggressive personalities stake out their turf. Although he'd been hired to fill the position of executive assistant (a position never formalized and never filled successfully despite several prior attempts), someone was already functioning in that role. From the first minute he attempted to do what he was hired to do, Jack was encroaching on territory Betty had already claimed as her own. So, right from the beginning, Betty was "scoping out" his vulnerabilities, looking for the most effective place to strike.

Because Jack didn't recognize Betty's personality type, he didn't anticipate the moves she was likely to make to maintain power. He assumed that all of her ostensible efforts to help and support him were sincere. Like many, He didn't really understand that there are characters very different from his own. Not knowing how to recognize a wolf or a wolf in sheep's clothing was his biggest vulnerability. Jack has since learned to recognize such types. Unfortunately, he had to learn about them the hard way.

Reactive Vs. Predatory Aggression

Betty's distinctive "style" of getting her way and hanging onto power illustrates a point about aggressive behavior that is all too often ignored by professionals. Aggression can be of two very different types: reactive and predatory (some researchers prefer the term "instrumental"). Reactive aggression is an emotional response to a threatening situation. It's not something we plan, it's something we spontaneously do when we are frightened to death and there's nowhere to run. The whole character of reactive aggression is different from predatory aggression. A presenter at a workshop I once attended[24] used an analogy I have found very useful. He pointed out that when a cat is faced with a threatening situation (e.g., a bulldog approaching), it exhibits certain stereotypic behaviors. First, it arches its back. It may show its claws. It may hiss. Its hair stands on end. Its emotions are right on the surface. Despite its fear, it focuses its eyes on the potential attacker and does everything possible to openly and obviously signal its preparedness to aggress in the hope the attacker will retreat and it won't have to fight. The "enemy" knows what might happen and gets the chance to run.

Predatory or instrumental aggression is very different. It's not an instantaneous reaction, it's a planned and deliberate initiative. It's also not primarily prompted by fear, but rather fueled by *desire*. The mode of behavior is different, too. When a cat is on the prowl (e.g., spots a mouse), it keeps low to the ground, hair undisturbed, is quiet and careful. It remains as calm and collected as possible as it prepares to pounce on its prey. The intended victim never sees what's coming. If it does, it's usually after it's too late.

When a cat is stalking a mouse for lunch, it would be ridiculous to assume that it is doing so out of fear of the mouse, is angry with the mouse, has "unresolved anger issues" in general, or is "acting-out" past trauma of victimization by a mouse, etc. Yet, these are precisely the kinds of assumptions many mental health professionals and laypersons alike make when they march predatory aggressors into anger management classes or fear of intimacy groups. It's hard for some people to understand the simple under-pinnings of predatory aggression and equally hard for them to accept that all creatures are capable of this type of aggressive conduct.

Popular wisdom would have it that Betty feared the loss of her job and "reacted" to the "threat" by getting rid of her enemy. But her behavior in the preceding story less resembles the startled cat and more resembles the cat on the prowl. As in all predatory aggression, Betty was not motivated by fear or any emotion other than desire. Just as the cat that simply wanted lunch, Betty's behavior reflected her appetite for power and status. Betty is crafty, clever and cunning when it comes to getting and keeping it. When she went after Jack, she was low to the ground, calm, collected, quiet, and never perceived as threatening before she struck. Jack never saw it coming.

chapter 6

THE IMPAIRED CONSCIENCE

Aggressive personalities don't like anyone pushing them to do what they don't want to do or stopping them from doing what they want to do. "No" is never an answer they accept. Because they so actively resist any constraints on their behavior or desires, they have trouble forming a healthy conscience.

Conscience can be conceptualized as a self-imposed barrier to an unchecked pursuit of personal goals. It's a person's internal set of "brakes." Aggressive personalities resist society's exhortation to install these brakes. They tend to *fight the socialization process* early on. If they're not too aggressively predisposed, and if they can see some benefit in self-restraint, they might internalize some inhibitions. But generally, any conscience they do form is likely to be significantly impaired. This is the heart of conscience development: **Internalization of a societal prohibition is the definitive act of *submission*.** Because all of the aggressive personalities *detest* and *resist* submission, they necessarily develop impaired consciences.

The conscience of covert-aggressives is uniquely impaired in several ways. By refraining from overt acts of hostility towards others, they manage to convince themselves and others they're not the ruthless people they are. They may observe the letter of a law but violate its spirit with ease. They may exhibit behavioral constraint when it's in their best interest, but they resist truly submitting themselves to any higher authority or set of principles. Many people have asked me if I'm really sure that covert-aggressives are as calculating and conniving as I describe them. "Maybe they just can't help it," they tell me or "they must do these things unconsciously." While some covert-aggressives are to some extent neurotic and therefore prone to deceiving themselves about their aggressive intentions, most of the covert-aggressives I've encountered have been primarily character disordered, striving primarily to conceal their true intentions and aggressive agendas from others. They may behave with civility and propriety when they're closely scrutinized or vulnerable. But when they believe they're immune from detection or retribution, it's an entirely different story. The following case is an example.

The Story of Mary Jane

Mary Jane was just about to give up. It was bad enough that her husband left her for a younger woman and that she had to raise her son alone. Now she was on her eleventh job interview, following five weeks of "We'll give you a call." She was desperate and this time she made no attempt to hide it. "Mr. Jackson," she pleaded, "if you hire me, I can promise you that I'll work harder than anyone else you've ever met. I need this job in the worst way."

When she started to work the next day, Mary Jane had more hope in her heart than she had in months. She was still feeling quite vulnerable, however. She had let Mr. Jackson know how desperate she was and never negotiated about starting salary or eventual opportunities for pay and position advancements. But Mr. Jackson knew she had little prior work experience but was willing to give her a chance. As far as she was concerned, that spoke well for him.

On those days that Mary Jane felt uncomfortable around her boss, she kept in mind how important her job was to her immediate security as well as her future. Even though it unnerved her somewhat when he leaned over her shoulder so closely or stared at her so intently, she was able to pass it off and keep her attention on her priorities. It just seemed to be his style. He was always being "friendly" with the female staff. Besides, he was quite vocal about being happily married and seemed to enjoy bragging on his wife and children when they visited the office.

It was only after a year or so without a pay increase and under the pressure of mounting duties that Mary Jane began to think she should have a serious talk with her boss. She had approached him before, of course. But she knew he was correct when he pointed out to her that despite her good work at his company, she had no real marketable skills and was fortunate to have the opportunity that she did. He also reminded her of the many times that he offered to work out some "special" arrangements with her to do some extra work for additional compensation without other staff members knowing, thus eliminating the possibility of destructive jealousy among her co-workers. However, the idea of meeting over dinners and working at his out-of-town retreat was unsettling to her. She never expressed her discomfort to him directly because she didn't want to offend him. Besides, she wasn't sure she had any legitimate reason to feel uneasy.

One day, when she was working late and there was nobody else around, Mary Jane decided to confront Mr. Jackson. She felt she just had to express her concern over the increasing work demands and the fact that, unlike others, she'd never gotten a raise. Maybe it was just the fact that it was just herself and her boss in that big empty building, but Mr. Jackson's whole demeanor seemed different. "I thought you were a sharp little gal," he blurted. "If you were willing to play your cards right, you could have just about anything you want." Mary Jane could feel the tension rising in her as she challenged him to be more specific. She expressed shock that he seemed to take no note of how much she had matured on the job and to what extent she had, with much dedication and gratitude, taken on increased responsibilities. "Don't flatter yourself!" he retorted. "There are plenty of others here who know what side their bread is buttered on! Some of them have been much more cooperative and you can see how far that has gotten them! For an entire year now, I've been waiting for you to see the light."

Mary Jane felt so used. She had also seen a glimpse of what she's always suspected but could never prove. Now that she had proof, there were no witnesses! Moreover, she was in a real trap. She knew Mr. Jackson was right when he pointed out how important it was for her to get a good reference from her one and only employer should she have the audacity to leave. Although she felt ashamed of herself, she still needed his financial support so desperately that she couldn't just walk out.

Manipulated and exploited, Mary Jane hated to see that smile on Mr. Jackson's face as he made his daily cruise through the secretarial cubicles, making those occasional stops to share his photos of his son or show off the new ring he purchased for his wife's birthday. It was that confident smile that finally made her quit. She just couldn't take it any more.

Getting Away with Murder

Covert-aggressives exploit situations in which they are well aware of the vulnerability of their victims. They are often very selective about the kinds of people with whom they will associate or work. They are particularly adept at finding and keeping others in a one-down position. They relish being in positions of power over others. It's my experience that how a person uses power is the most reliable test of their character. Mary Jane's boss is undoubtedly character-disordered. He is a channeled-aggressive as well as covert-aggressive personality. Although he appeared to be the kind of a guy who would give a person a break, he is without a conscience. He counted on Mary Jane's vulnerability to give him advantage. Believing that he was immune from detection and "punishment" for his behavior, he eventually allowed his true character to show.

The Conscience but not the Record of a Sociopath

Mr. Jackson has virtually no regard for the rights and needs of others. Some would be tempted to label him antisocial or even sociopathic. But he is not about the daily business of working against society. He has never broken any major laws, and through his business enterprise he is one of his community's members actively building a better society. By definition, therefore, he is not antisocial. But we do need some labels to describe his callous disregard for others and his willingness to manipulate and exploit them. His conscience is obviously impaired but we don't have enough indication that he is so devoid of all conscience that we can rightfully call him psychopathic or sociopathic. But he certainly meets all of the criteria outlined in Chapter 1 for a channeled-aggressive and covert-aggressive personality.

The Root of Mr. Jackson's "Evil"

There are those who suggest that people like Mr. Jackson are "evil."[25] But what is it about him that makes him evil? Is he evil just because he is aggressive? Is aggression in itself a "sin?" Aggression toward others can cause pain and misery, so it's tempting to think of it as evil. But not all of Mr. Jackson's aggressiveness has resulted in pain toward others. His appropriately channeled aggression is responsible for the success of his business and the financial well-being of several employees. But Mr. Jackson has failed to fully "own" and responsibly restrain his aggressive tendencies. When it comes to getting what he wants from others, he places few limits on himself. He knows how to maintain appearances and how to cover his tracks. He even knows how to protect himself if caught. So, the "evil" in Mr. Jackson is that although he knows how to look good, he has never made the commitment to **be good** by accepting need for and doing the hard work of disciplining his aggression.

One-Down Positions

There are times in everyone's life when they are inescapably in a one-down position and ripe to be manipulated. Mr. Jackson didn't have to use many of the usual tactics to manipulate Mary Jane. He was well aware of her vulnerability and used it to his advantage. He let her sink deeper and deeper into a one-down position with respect to her peers and then offered her a way out that he thought she was too disadvantaged to refuse. This was his primary manipulation tactic.

Mary Jane might have spent more time evaluating the kind of person for whom she was going to work, but she really needed a job. She was in an unavoidable position of vulnerability and ripe for manipulation and exploitation. Her experience taught her some important things about the hazards of being in positions of vulnerability and the kinds of things to look for in the character of those who might easily take advantage of her when in such a position.

ABUSIVE, MANIPULATIVE RELATIONSHIPS

Covert-aggressives use a variety of ploys to keep their partners in a subordinate position in relationships. Of course, it takes two people to make a relationship work and each party must assume responsibility for their own behavior. But covert-aggressives are often so expert at exploiting the weaknesses and emotional insecurities of others that almost anyone can be duped. Persons in abusive relationships with covert-aggressives are often initially seduced by their smooth-talking, outwardly charming ways. By the time they realize their partner's true character, they've usually put a significant emotional investment into trying to make the relationship work. This makes it very hard to simply walk away.

The Woman Who Couldn't Walk Away

Janice felt guilty for what she was about to do. She'd been feeling guilty for a few days now. She was going to leave Bill. She had no plans to divorce him, but she wanted the time and the personal space to sort things out. She wasn't sure why, exactly, but she felt that somehow she wouldn't be able to think clearly if she stayed in the same house with him. So, she decided to get away for a while. While she was out of town visiting her sister, Janice realized just what a relief it was to be away from so many of the usual family conflicts. It wasn't that she hated helping her twice-divorced daughter raise her fatherless child. It wasn't that she wanted to abandon her son, who, after dropping out of college and getting fired from another job, needed a place to stay. But she always seemed to be giving, giving, giving, just to make things work. Now, drained and tired, she needed to do something for herself. She was relieved, but, as always, feeling guilty.

Mostly, Janice was feeling guilty about leaving Bill. She's heard him talk about the pressure he was under at work. And yes, he'd been drinking again, but not like in the past. Perhaps Bill had a point when he complained she hadn't been giving him the attention and emotional support that he needed lately. Maybe she had been spending too much money at a time when they could least afford it, just as Bill said. But she didn't feel much like supporting him in recent days because of the way he had been acting. She felt guilty about that, too.

Janice felt most guilty when she thought about what might happen to Bill if she left for good. She'd tried to leave him several times before. It was always such a setback for his "recovery." She learned all about chemical dependency from the times she pressured Bill to seek treatment in a 28-day program. But she saw some logic in Bill's insistence that he didn't need counseling, treatment, or A.A. meetings because, as he explained, his drinking was never excessive when things were going well at work, with the kids, and when she was supportive of him. Bill was right, she thought, to point out that he only "relapsed" into heavier drinking or did those things the drinking "causes" (i.e. the rages, philandering and cheating) during those times when she was thinking of walking out on him.

Despite her usual guilt, Janice was convinced that this time would be different. This time, Bill said he understood. He'd said that before, but now he was sounding more sincere. He told her that if she needed some time to herself that she should take it. After all, he still loved her. Bill told her not to worry that problems were mounting at work, that the kids seemed to be needing a lot of attention, or that he'd had episodes of heavy drinking again. He understood that she needed to look after herself. Maybe, he told her, she would find herself missing him as much as he was already starting to miss her.

At first, with the ordeal of moving into an apartment and securing work, Janice barely had time to think about Bill or the kids. Bill didn't call much at first, just as he said he wouldn't. He explained that the only reason he'd been calling more frequently lately was because he knew she would want to know what was happening with the kids.

On his last call, Bill's voice sounded shaky and his speech a little slurred as he told Janice not to worry about him, his temptations to drink, or the possibility that he might be losing his job soon. He insisted he was handling the "deep pain" of their separation and the problems with their children as best as anyone could all by himself. Within a few weeks, Janice was feeling very guilty.

The day the call came from the hospital Janice was so confused. "An overdose?," she asked herself, "How can I possibly feel angry about somebody taking an overdose?" Unsure about the legitimacy of her anger, she eventually became mired in her guilt and shame. After seeing Bill lying in that hospital bed with that tube pumping his stomach, it didn't matter to her that the doctor said he hadn't really taken enough of his pain pills to do himself any serious damage. She just looked at him, imagining the pain and anguish that must have "driven" him to do such a thing. Once again, she began to believe that she'd been too selfish.

Bill needed her, she thought. That made her feel good. It always made her feel worthwhile to be needed. He reached for her hand. "I didn't think you'd come," he said, "but I'm glad you're with me. For a while, I thought I couldn't make it," he added. "Now that you're back, I'm sure I can."

The Perfect Victim

When Janice got the call from the hospital, she initially felt angry. She didn't understand why, however. Her gut was telling her she was being abused but Bill hadn't done anything overtly cruel to her. So, she didn't grant legitimacy to her feelings. Her anger was soon overshadowed by her customary feelings of guilt. As a result, she came to see Bill as only a victim and not a manipulator. As she goes back for more of the same, her guilt will pass but feelings of frustration and sadness will soon rise. It's an endless, vicious cycle that she's been through many times.

Bill uses the tactic of *playing the victim role* with consummate precision. He knows how to engender sympathy and invite others to feel like the bad guy for "deserting" him in his hour of need. And Janice has all of the right personality characteristics to fall for this tactic hook, line and sinker. She hates to think of herself as the bad guy. She doesn't like to hurt anyone. In fact she's one of those caretakers who's much more concerned about everyone else's welfare than her own. When she thinks she's being selfish, she's riddled with guilt and shame. So, when Bill combines the tactics of playing the victim with *guilt-tripping* and *shaming* techniques, Janice is ready to take the fall.

Bill is also expert at *externalizing the blame* for his behavior. He asserts he only cheats and has rages when he's drinking and he only drinks when Janice emotionally neglects him. He has two perfect scapegoats: Janice and booze. The only thing more destructive than the fact that he scapegoats is the fact that Janice falls prey to this ploy.

The Slot Machine Syndrome

There's a syndrome that can develop in abusive, manipulative relationships that prompts a victim to stay even when they've often thought about leaving. I call it the Slot Machine Syndrome. Anyone who's played one of those "one-armed bandits" knows that it's difficult to stop pulling the lever even when you're losing pretty badly. There are primarily four reasons why a person can get trapped in this syndrome. First, there's the appeal of the "jackpot." People often jump at the chance to get a lot of something that's very valuable to them for what initially appears a relatively small investment. Second, whether or not you will get anything for your efforts depends only on the degree to which you are willing to "respond" (behaviorists call this a ratio schedule of reinforcement). With a slot machine, you have to do a lot of "responding" (investing) to even have a chance at winning. Third, every now and then, a "cherry" (or, some similar small jackpot) appears and you "win" a little something. This reinforces the idea that your investment is not for naught and that "winning" a larger payoff is really possible if you just keep investing. Fourth, after you've been worn down by the machine's "abuse" and are tempted to walk away, you're faced with a most difficult dilemma. If you leave, you leave behind a substantial investment. You not only have to walk away from your "abuser," but from a huge chunk of yourself. To disengage with nothing to show for your time and energy but a broken spirit is hard to do. You're tempted to delude yourself by saying: "If I just put in one more quarter..."

In the early days of their relationship, Bill was very attentive and flattering to Janice. To Janice, these were signs that he really approved of her. She highly valued this apparent approval. Soon, however, it became clear that Janice would get few messages of approval and virtually no emotional support from Bill unless she invested a great deal of herself in tending to his wishes. Every now and then, when she was tending to all of his needs, he'd give her a little of the approval she wanted. Over the years she invested a lot of herself securing those tiny little "payoffs." The syndrome left her with the illusion of control while she was being taken to the cleaners. But now that she's invested so much, it's very difficult for her to realistically consider walking away. Besides, if she does leave and admits that she's made a big mistake for several years, she's likely to feel ashamed of herself. Shame and guilt are very big issues for Janice and make it even more difficult for her to leave.

Aggressive Personalities in "Recovery"

The case of Janice and Bill and many subsequent similar cases have taught me that the central tenets of traditional "recovery" models designed to treat true chemical addiction are detrimental when applied to chemically abusing individuals with aggressive (or covert-aggressive) personality disorders. These models often prompt us to view an abusive and emotionally *independent* personality as a victim and as *dependent*. The traditional model would view Bill as chemically dependent and Janice as *co-dependent*. In recent years, zealous professional advocates have expanded the "co-dependency model" to include any and all types of interpersonal dependence. Within such an exaggerated framework, *everyone* is to some extent co-dependent. Now, there are cases of real dependency and co-dependency, but they are not as common as many claim. In many more troubled relationships, there is an emotionally independent, abusive party and another party who is insecure and struggling with excessive emotional dependence.

Bill is an actively-independent (aggressive) personality and a victimizer. Janice is not co-dependent but just plain dependent, and the ideal victim. Bill's actively-independent coping style is reflected in just about everything he does. He has always worked for himself because he detests having to answer to anyone else. When he and his associates play golf, he always drives the cart. Despite what we might think about the long-term consequences of his drinking, he always intends to take very good care of himself. He carefully set up a secret bank account to finance some of his "business trips" with his cohorts and maintains a hideaway for his escapades with a long list of female acquaintances. Although his tactic of playing the needy husband makes it appear he depends on Janice, his desire to keep her is largely pragmatic. He has substantial wealth and property and doesn't want a fair divorce settlement. He would rather keep Janice in tow and do all of his philandering on the sly. Make no mistake, Bill is a very *independent* guy.

Now, a case can be made that chemical dependency is a free-standing condition that is unrelated to emotional independence or dependence. But my experience is that abusive personalities show similar patterns of behavior with all of the "objects" in their lives with which they have some kind of relationship, *including their drugs of choice*. Bill has never met the criteria for genuine chemical dependency (addiction). His drinking pattern is more the pattern of a cyclic *substance abuser*. Judging from the apparent evidence, Bill is both a substance and a people abuser.

It's my experience (and the experience of a growing number of professionals)[26] that people with aggressive personality disorders do poorly in treatments that view or treat them as dependent in any way. When Janice tried to force Bill into treatment in the past (he went to appease her) he was admitted to a typical addictive disorders unit at a local hospital. These chemical dependency treatment programs based on a 12-step model of recovery are anathema to all aggressive personalities. To admit that they are in any way powerless challenges their deepest convictions. To believe that a higher power holds the key to their recovery is incompatible with their inflated self-regard. That they should submit their wills and conduct to a higher power is truly aversive. To ask them to think of themselves as in any way dependent when all their lives they have prized their active interpersonal independence is unreasonable. If pressured into treatment, they may say all of the right things in order to get others off their backs (this is the tactic of *giving assent*) but they rarely accept the central tenets of these types of programs in their hearts.

As is often the case with submissive personalities, Janice was initially attracted to Bill because his confident, independent, style made her feel safe when she was with him. She never thought much of herself or her ability to take care of herself. Dependent upon someone else's approval and support for any sense of self-worth, she was chronically vulnerable to exploitation.

Janice's behavior more accurately fits the classical model of addiction. The central tenets of traditional recovery programs are tailor-made for *her*. With her sense of self-worth dependent on Bill's assertions that he values her, she is *addicted* to him. Moreover, she cannot give up what has become destructive to her because she has habituated to the painful aspects of the relationship and still gets some things out of it that she desperately needs. In her increasing tolerance it takes more and more abuse for her to experience enough pain to want to break the addiction. When she attempts to disengage, she experiences psychological withdrawal. Tolerance and withdrawal symptoms are the hallmark features of a genuine addiction. People like Janice often do well in Al-Anon or in so-called "co-dependency" groups because unlike their abusive partners, their behavior patterns are very compatible with a dependency model and, as the model predicts, sometimes they hit an emotional bottom and want out of pain badly enough to take the "steps" necessary to "recover."

The Bottom Line in Abusive Relationships

An attendee at one of my workshops asked me why, if Bill wasn't at least to some degree co-dependent on Janice, he fought so hard to not lose her. My answer was that Bill, as an aggressive personality simply hates to lose. Losing means giving up a position of dominance and power. And no matter what relationship he's in, Bill seeks to be on top and in control. In any abusive relationship, the other person is never the real object of the aggressor's desire, the position is. Every time Janice feels empowered enough to even think about leaving, the balance of power is upset. That's when Bill goes to war. He doesn't fight to keep the woman he loves, wants or needs. He fights to stay on top. As a disordered character, Bill also tends to view Janice as more of a possession. As such, she is not free to have a life of her own—or even worse—a better life with someone else. As far as he is concerned, she is his property, and any move toward independence on her part is seen as a rejection of him and his "right" to dominance.

THE MANIPULATIVE CHILD

For many years professionals have focused on how children's fears and insecurities influence their personality development. But they haven't given much attention to how children learn to discipline and channel their aggressive instincts. It seems that when it comes to examining and dealing with the truth about why and how children fight, and how the degree of their aggressiveness shapes their personalities, professionals have exhibited a major case of denial.

Children naturally fight for what they want. Early in their social development they fight openly and often physically. For most children, this strategy proves unsuccessful and invites substantial social sanction. If their parents are skilled enough at discipline, their social environments benign enough, and if the children themselves are malleable enough, most children learn to modulate their overtly aggressive tendencies and will explore other strategies for winning life's battles. Along the way, many will discover the emotional "buttons" their parents and others possess that, when pressed, prompt them to back down or give ground in a conflict. They also learn the things that they can say or do (or fail to say or do) that will keep their "opponents" in the dark, off balance or on the defensive. These children then learn to fight covertly.

As the result of many social factors (permissiveness, indulgence, abuse, neglect, and lack of accountability), it seems that there is an increasing number of overtly aggressive and covertly aggressive (manipulative) children these days. My perspective may be biased because about half of my work in the early years was with emotionally and behaviorally disturbed children, adolescents and their families. However, I'm constantly impressed by the number of cases I see in which a child has managed to gain inordinate power in the family as a result of learning all too well the tactics of manipulation. The following story is based on one of these cases.

Amanda the Tyrannical Child

Jenny felt pretty nervous sitting in the waiting room. She was so worried about her daughter. Amanda's words: "You must think I'm crazy, because only crazy people go to head-shrinks!" and "You're always thinking bad things about me," kept running through her mind. Worried about how Amanda might react to having to see yet another professional, Jenny came alone for the first visit.

"I'm very concerned about my daughter," she explained. "She must have very low self-esteem." Asked to explain further, she told about the time she took away extra-curricular activity privileges from Amanda unless she began turning in her homework. She remembered how Amanda sobbed and screamed: "You think I meant to forget it, that I'm stupid, and now you're being mean to me. Everybody hates me, my teacher hates me and now you hate me, too!" and hid herself in her room.

"I didn't mean to hurt her feelings," Jenny noted. "I'm sure she already feels bad enough about herself. I tried to tell her I was just trying to help her be more responsible about her work and that it was only her behavior I was upset about. But she wouldn't even speak to me until I told her I'd hold off punishing her until I had a chance to talk with her teacher. That seemed to cheer her up a bit."

Jenny related how there might be some truth to Amanda's constant complaint that the teachers at school have it in for her. "She did have quite a reputation for a while, but Amanda's really different now," Jenny explained. "Until last year she was bigger than her brother Joey, and for that matter, many of the kids at school. She used to hit Joey and bully him and was suspended for fighting on the school bus. Her father and I used to deal with her for that all of the time. But now the other kids have caught up to her and even though he's younger, Joey's undergone a growth spurt and is bigger than she is now. He doesn't lord it over her, but Amanda doesn't treat him the way she used to."

Jenny shared her concern that Amanda must feel insecure and, therefore, overly sensitive to the things the kids at school say. She related how Amanda frequently tells her how the others pick on her and "make her mad," and that the teachers are always singling her out as a behavior problem while never seeming to notice the others picking on her. Amanda told her about this several times. "In some ways I think Amanda is as insecure and lacking in self-esteem as I was as a child," Jenny pointed out. "I always got depressed when I didn't get the support I needed, and one of the counselors we've seen in the past thought Amanda might be depressed." Jenny told of the number of times that

Amanda had threatened to run away from home, how she said she might as well be dead and how she wanted to go live with her father, because "he understands" her. "I think she feels helpless and depressed, don't you? I think she's felt that way ever since the divorce. Maybe I made a mistake divorcing Amanda's father two years ago. I tried to understand his insecurities too, but I couldn't take the beatings anymore. I want Amanda to be happy, and I don't want her to hate me. Do you think we can help her? We have to do something. Today, the principal called and threatened to suspend her. I begged him not to until I got her some help."

A Bully by Any Other Name

Amanda doesn't fight like she used to fight. She doesn't have the physical size and strength advantage that she once had. But Amanda is still a fighter and quite a bully. Only the way she fights has changed. She has scoped out her mother's weaknesses, and knows what tactics to use to bring Jenny to submission.

Like most people, Jenny can more readily recognize aggressive behavior when it's open, direct and physical. In fact, she dealt much differently with her ex-husband and her daughter when they were fighting overtly. But because she doesn't see the aggression in Amanda's present behavior, she inadvertently enables it. As a result, Amanda is becoming quite the manipulator. Ironically, because Jenny can't tell when Amanda is fighting and doesn't know how to stand up to her, she's being abused all over again.

I remember when Jenny first attempted to describe Amanda's frequent verbal attacks. "I can't say anything to her," she complained, "she gets so *defensive*." I asked, "Tell me what you mean when you say 'defensive.'" "Well," Jenny explained, "she starts shouting at me—telling me what a bad mother I am—threatening to do terrible things." I commented inquisitively, "It's interesting that you would describe these relentless verbal assaults as some kind of 'defensive' behavior. From what you've told me, it seems that whenever you ask something of Amanda she doesn't want to do or observe something about her behavior you want her to change, she quickly goes on the offensive." "I guess that's a different way to look at it," was Jenny's reply. "But why would she go on the attack if she wasn't feeling threatened?"

The Root of the Problem

As is all too common, Jenny's been looking for the underlying causes of Amanda's behavior. Based on the psychology she's familiar with, she believes that some fear or insecurity must be at the root of Amanda's problem. Apparently, when she was still married, she tried to find underlying reasons for her husband's abusive behavior, too. Now, Amanda may be struggling with some fears and insecurities. She may even have some unresolved issues about her parents' divorce. Maybe she's still angry. Maybe she blames her mother. But all of the frustrations in her life that "invite" her to aggress are not the problem. Her personality has become the problem. She has begun to solidify a lifestyle of fighting too much and too underhandedly. She uses *guilt-tripping, playing the victim, blaming others*, and *making veiled threats* as her preferred ways to attack anyone getting in the way of what she wants.

Correctly Identifying Victim and Victimizer

In this story, Jenny wanted to "help" Amanda. But when they first came to see me, Amanda neither needed nor was she seeking help. She did need correction (i.e. corrective behavioral and emotional experience), but not help. Jenny was the real victim and she desperately needed help. Amanda required much correction of her thinking and behavior patterns to bring her to the point where she recognized the need for, solicited and truly accepted any help.

I cannot overly stress why traditional viewpoints about human behavior fail so miserably when it comes to understanding and dealing with the disturbed character. Amanda doesn't need insight. She doesn't need "help." She doesn't need to uncover unconscious fears or insecurities. She doesn't need to overcome poor self-esteem. In short, she needs nothing that traditional approaches offer. She needs correction. She needs limit-setting. She needs to be confronted about her distorted thinking patterns and attitudes and needs to correct her covertly aggressive conduct. Her inflated self-image needs correcting also. This is the work of cognitive-behavioral therapy.

Children aren't equipped to handle a lot of power. They don't have the emotional maturity or necessary life experience to wield power responsibly. Through her manipulative expertise, Amanda had corralled far too much power within her family. Empowering Jenny in her dealings with Amanda was crucial for restoring the mental and emotional health of both of them.

Some Important Words about Self-Esteem

Like many, Jenny assumed that Amanda might be suffering from low self-esteem. It's hard for her to imagine how anyone could say the things Amanda said and not lack self-esteem. Even when her gut told her that Amanda was acting "too big for her britches," she assumed it must be a compensation for feeling badly about herself.

Self-esteem is not a unipolar attribute. A person can just as easily have too much as too little self-esteem. And, a person who is acting "too big for their britches" is not always compensating for an underlying insecurity (neurotics sometimes are, but character-disordered individuals usually aren't). Someone who has managed to corral inordinate power and thinks, from all immediate evidence, that they're invincible can easily come to overly esteem themselves. This is especially true in Amanda's case and is reflected in her confident drive to usurp ever more power at home and in school.

The Difference Between Self-Esteem and Self-Respect

It's important to make a distinction between the concepts of self-esteem and self-respect. The word esteem derives from a word meaning to estimate. Self-esteem is the intuitive "estimate" we make of our worth based on an assessment of our innate talents, abilities and the success we've had at getting what we want in life. Individuals who know what they have going for themselves and are confident about their ability to get what they want can overly esteem themselves while never developing any legitimate self-respect. The word respect literally means to "look back." Self-respect arises, therefore, out of a favorable retrospective assessment of one's personal effort, commitment to socially desirable goals and, if luck would have it, achievement. To put it more simply, our sense of self-esteem derives from what we know we have, while our sense of self-respect derives from what we've done with what we've been given.

Amanda's sense of self-esteem is, no doubt, out of balance. Not viewing her mother, her teachers or any authority figures as forces to be respected, Amanda thinks entirely too much of herself. And, she thinks that she's "winning" because she's successful in using her talents to get her way. But because in the long-run, she is likely to develop a history of social failures, she will have a hard time developing self-respect.

Parents and others sometimes inadvertently reinforce the things that lead kids to overly esteem themselves. They praise them for their intelligence, their looks, their talents, in short, for all of the things for which the child cannot legitimately claim credit. That is, there is no acknowledgment of a "high power" (i.e. nature, God, or whatever endowing entity you choose to recognize) as responsible for these fortunate "accidents" of birth. Further, parents will frequently praise children for achievement. This is okay if other things are taken into consideration, but frequently there is no recognition of the fortuitousness of circumstances and the opportunities that usually play a significant role in achievement.

Unfortunately, parents frequently fail to stroke their children for the one thing for which they can truly claim sole credit: their willingness to work. "Sweat" alone is worthy of praise and its appreciation is essential to a healthy sense of self-respect. This is so important to remember. It's not what people are given that we should praise, or what they manage to secure, but what they do with their talents and abilities and how hard they work to make an honest, responsible contribution to society. Unfortunately, I've met far too many young people who think a whole lot of themselves but have virtually no self-respect.

A Parent's Biggest Fear

At a deeply unconscious level, many parents sense the active-independence some children possess. They know that these kinds of children don't seem to need others in the ways most other children do. They also know that the more they push them, restrain them or try to limit them, the more the child threatens to pull away. So, sometimes parents fall into the trap of trying to appease such a child so as not to run the risk of losing them.

Ironically, once Jenny became more empowered in her dealing with Amanda, two important things happened. First, Amanda came to believe that there are entities in her life that are stronger, wiser and more capable than herself, gaining some much needed humility. Second, learning that it was sometimes in her best interest to accept guidance and direction from her mother, she found herself increasingly more dependent upon her. Her increased dependence is not the unhealthy dependence of a dependent personality but a necessary counterbalancing of her former excessive independence. Jenny's increased empowerment didn't result in her worst fear coming true. One of her fondest dreams came true. Instead of losing a daughter, she gained one.

PART II

Dealing Effectively with Manipulative People

RECOGNIZING THE TACTICS OF MANIPULATION AND CONTROL

Defense Mechanisms and Offensive Tactics

Almost everyone is familiar with the term *defense mechanism*. Genuine defense mechanisms are the almost reflexive mental behaviors we sometimes employ to shield ourselves from the "threat" of some type of emotional pain. More specifically, ego defense mechanisms are mental behaviors people might use to "defend" their self-images from anxiety associated with societal "invitations" to feel ashamed or guilty about something. There are many different kinds of ego defenses, several of which are well known and have made their way into common discourse.

The use of defense mechanisms is one of the cardinal tenets of traditional or psychodynamic approaches to understanding human behavior. In fact, these approaches have always tended to distinguish the various personality types, at least in part, by the types of ego defenses they are believed to most commonly use. As discussed briefly earlier, there are some characteristics of traditional approaches to understanding human behavior and personality that do not really help us understand the disturbed character. Traditional approaches assert that people necessarily experience guilt, shame, and anxiety when they do something wrong. They also claim that people defend themselves against "threats" to their self-image by using the automatic behaviors we call defense mechanisms. Finally, they maintain that people do so *unconsciously*.

Traditional models of human behavior and personality are not helpful when it comes to understanding the character disturbed individual. When disturbed characters engage in certain behaviors, some of which we have often called defense mechanisms, they don't do so primarily to protect against emotional pain, guilt or shame. Nor do they do so to keep a feared event from happening. Rather, disturbed characters engage in these behaviors *primarily* to ensure that some desired event does indeed happen, to manipulate and control others, and to solidify their resistance to accepting or internalizing social norms. They use them as vehicles to keep doing what society says we shouldn't do and, as a result, they don't develop a healthy sense of guilt or shame. Furthermore, for the most part they engage in these behaviors *consciously* even though habitual use prompts them to be employed nearly reflexively. So, many of the behaviors we have traditionally thought of as defense mechanisms more rightfully should be thought of as responsibility-avoidance behaviors and *tactics of manipulation and control* when they are employed by disturbed characters.

Let's take the mechanism of denial, for example. Almost everyone has heard someone say something like: "Sure, he has a problem, but he's *in denial* about it." Most of the time, this term is misused. The true defense mechanism of denial is a *psychological state* unconsciously employed to protect a person from unbearable emotional pain. Take the case of Agnes, an elderly woman still in relatively good health who has just been told by doctors at the hospital that the stroke her husband of 40 years has just suffered is critical and means he likely won't recover. Paul has been her lover and beloved partner for most of her adult life and she is not prepared to lose him. She faces the prospect of being alone and without his steadfast support. Life without him, she thinks, would be unbearable. So, despite the fact the brainwave charts are flat, she stays by his side, day after day, holding his hand, talking to him, and insisting to those who tell her otherwise that she knows he'll make it—he always has. This woman is "in denial." She is not intentionally doing so, but unconsciously she is protecting herself against the sudden and unbearable experience of the intense grief she will experience when reality eventually sets in. Over time, when she is more psychologically prepared to suffer the trauma, her denial mechanism will break down. When it finally does, she will be without the protection that kept her from the experience of pain, and what will burst forth is an avalanche of emotion.

Contrast the aforementioned scenario with the case of Jeff, a character-disturbed adolescent called out by his junior high hall monitor for bullying an underclassman by shoving his books on the floor. "What?" he retorts. "I didn't do anything!" He is denying the behavior, but is he in a psychological state of denial? No! The classical perspective suggests: 1) underneath the pretense, he feels bad about what he did, 2) to *defend* himself against unbearable feelings of shame and/or guilt he simply can't admit to himself or anyone else what he did; and 3) he consciously has no idea what he's doing. These are dangerous presuppositions, but ones that laypersons and many professionals frequently make. They are also assumptions that, when it comes to the disturbed character, are *completely erroneous*. The more accurate perspective is that Jeff is fairly lacking in guilt, shame, or anxiety about his behavior, which is why he so unhesitatingly committed the acts in the first place. What is also likely is that he hasn't made the commitment to deal with people in a non-aggressive way. Although other people aren't comfortable with his ways, he is. Because he has likely been chastised many times before for his problem behaviors, he's well aware that others view it as unacceptable. However, he's not prepared to submit himself to the standard of conduct others want him to adopt. He is also very aware of the likely consequences the hall monitor has in store for him. He may not want to face those consequences just as much as he doesn't want to change his style. So, his best bet is to try and convince the hall monitor that she is in error, that she didn't see what she thought she saw, that she has him judged all wrong, that she should back off. In short, when Jeff is denying, he's *not defending* in any way, he's mainly *fighting*. He's not in a psychological state, he's *employing a tactic*, and he's very aware of what he's doing. The tactic he's using is often called denial, but it's really just a simple case of *lying*. He's lying for the reasons people commonly lie: to get out of trouble. Proof positive could come when the hall monitor calls two or three other witnesses in front of him and they all verify what the monitor saw. Jeff may then say something like "Okay, okay. Maybe I shoved him a little. But he had it coming. He's been bugging me all week." Now, the traditionalists would say he's "come out of his denial." But unlike Helen, we don't see what we usually see when someone truly comes out of such a psychological state. *We don't see pain.* We don't see Jeff break down with grief. Instead, we see him making only a half-hearted admission and he continues to adamantly fight submission to the principle we want him to adopt. We see neither signs of shame nor guilt. We see only signs of defiance.

A most important thing to remember about Jeff's behavior is that although he lied quickly, automatically, and likely out of long-standing habit, he didn't do so unconsciously. *He knew what he was doing.* Acting innocent and denying something horrible so vehemently that your "accuser" begins to doubt the legitimacy of their complaint, is, from Jeff's abundant experience, an effective combat tool. It has gotten him out of trouble before, and he hopes it will work again. Remember, behaviors that are habitual and automatic are not the same thing as behaviors that are unconscious.

All character-disordered individuals, especially aggressive personalities, use a variety of mental behaviors and interpersonal maneuvers to help ensure they get what they want. The behaviors soon to be enumerated in this chapter simultaneously accomplish several things that can lead to victimization. Firstly, they help conceal the aggressive intent of the person using them. Secondly, their use frequently puts others on the defensive. Thirdly, their habitual use reinforces the user's dysfunctional but preferred way of dealing with the world. They obstruct any chance that the aggressor will accept and submit to an important social principle at stake, and thus change their ways. Lastly, because most people don't know how to correctly interpret the behaviors, they are effective tools to exploit, manipulate, abuse, and control others. If you're one of those persons more familiar with traditional psychological models, you may tend to view a person using one of these behaviors as being "on the defensive." But viewing someone who's in the act of aggressing as being defensive in any sense is a major set-up for victimization. Recognizing that when a person uses the behaviors soon to be described is primarily a person on the offensive mentally prepares you for the decisive action you might need to take to avoid being run over.

It's not possible to list all the tactics a good manipulator is capable of using to hoodwink or gain advantage over others. But the automatic mental behaviors and interpersonal maneuvers enumerated below are some of the more popular weapons in the arsenal of disturbed characters in general, aggressive personalities in particular, and especially covert-aggressives. It is important to remember that when people display these behaviors, they are at that very moment *fighting*. They are fighting against the values or standards of conduct they know others want them to adopt or internalize. They are also fighting to overcome resistance in others and to have their way.

Covert-aggressive individuals are especially adept at using these tactics to conceal their aggressive intentions while simultaneously throwing their opponents on the defensive. When people are on the defensive, their thoughts tend to become more confused, they tend to engage in more self-doubt, and they feel the urge to retreat. Using these tactics increases the chances manipulators will get their way and gain advantage over their victims. Sometimes, a tactic is used in isolation. More often, however, a skilled manipulator will throw so many of them at you at once that you might not really realize how badly you've been manipulated until it's too late.

Minimization—This tactic is a unique kind of denial coupled with rationalization. When using this maneuver, the aggressor is attempting to assert that his behavior isn't really as harmful or irresponsible as someone else may be claiming. It's the aggressor's attempt to make a molehill out of a mountain. The use of minimization clearly illustrates the difference between the neurotic individual and the disturbed character. Neurotics frequently make mountains out of molehills, or "catastrophize." The disturbed character frequently trivializes the nature of his wrongdoing. Manipulators do this to make a person who might confront them feel they've been overly harsh in their criticism or unjust in their appraisal of a situation.

In the story of Janice and Bill, Bill *minimized* his substance use problem by insisting he didn't have much of a drinking problem and asserting that binges occurred *only* when he was very stressed or feeling unsupported by Janice. Janice initially bought into this minimization, saying to herself that because his drinking wasn't always unbearable, his substance use pattern wasn't that serious.

I've encountered hundreds of examples over the years of aggressive personalities of all types minimizing the nature and impact of their aggressive conduct. "Maybe I touched her once, but I didn't hit her." "I pushed her a little, but I didn't leave any marks," they might say. They frequently use two "four-letter words" I forbid in therapy: *just* and *only*. The story is always the same. What they mean to do is convince me that I would be wrong to conclude that their behavior was really as wrong as they know I suspect. Minimization is not primarily the way they make themselves feel better about what they did, it's primarily the way they try to manipulate my impression of them. They don't want me to see them as a person who behaves like a thug. Remember, they are most often comfortable with their aggressive personality style, so their primary objective is to get me to believe that there's nothing wrong with the kind of person they are.

Lying—It's hard to tell when a person is lying at the time they're doing it. Fortunately, there are times when the truth will out because circumstances don't bear out somebody's story. But there are times when you don't know you've been deceived until it's too late. One way to minimize the chances that someone will put one over on you is to remember that because aggressive personalities of all types will generally stop at nothing to get what they want, you can expect them to lie and cheat. Another thing to remember is that manipulators—covert-aggressive personalities that they are—are prone to lie in subtle, covert ways. Someone was well aware of the many ways there are to lie when they suggested that court oaths charge a person to tell "the truth, the whole truth, and nothing but the truth." Manipulators and other disturbed characters have refined lying to nearly an art form.

It's very important to remember that disturbed characters of all sorts lie frequently—sometimes just for sport—and lie readily, even when the truth would easily suffice. **Lying by omission** is a very subtle form of lying that manipulators use. So is lying by *distortion*. Manipulators will withhold a significant amount of the truth from you or distort essential elements the truth to keep you in the dark. I have treated individuals who have lied most egregiously by reciting a litany of true facts! How does someone lie by saying only true things? They do so by leaving out facts essential to knowing the bigger picture or "whole story."

One of the most subtle forms of distortion is being deliberately vague. This is a favorite tactic of manipulators. They will carefully craft their stories so that you form the impression that you've been given information *but leave out essential details that would have otherwise made it possible for you to know the larger truth.*

In the story of Al and Don, Al didn't tell the whole truth when Don inquired about the safety of his job. It was a smooth, calculated *omission* and a damaging lie. He was deliberately vague about the company's plans. He may have even considered that Don would eventually learn the whole truth, but only after it was too late to thwart his plan.

Denial—As previously mentioned, this is when the aggressor refuses to admit that they've done something harmful or hurtful when they clearly have. It's a way they lie (to themselves as well as others) about their aggressive intentions. This "Who... Me?" tactic invites the victim to feel unjustified in confronting the aggressor about the inappropriateness of a behavior. It's also the way the aggressor gives him/herself permission to keep right on doing what they want to do. Again, this denial is *not* the same kind of denial that a person who has just lost a loved one and can't quite bear to accept the pain and reality of the loss engages in. That type of denial really is mostly a "defense" against unbearable hurt and anxiety. The tactic of denial is not primarily a "defense" but a maneuver the aggressor uses to get others to back off, back down or maybe even feel guilty themselves for

117

insinuating he's doing something wrong.

In the story of James the minister, James' denial of his ruthless ambition is massive. He denied he was hurting and neglecting his family. He especially denied he was aggressively pursuing any personal agenda. On the contrary, he cast himself as the humble servant to an honorable cause. He managed to convince several people (and maybe even himself) of the nobility and purity of his intentions. But underneath it all, James knew he was being dishonest. This fact is borne out in his reaction to the threat of not getting a seat on the Elders' Council if his marital problems worsened. When James learned he might not get what he was so aggressively pursuing after all, he had an interesting "conversion' experience. All of a sudden, he decided he could put aside the Lord's bidding for a weekend and he might really need to devote more time to his marriage and family. James' eyes weren't opened by the pastor's words. He always kept his awareness high about what might hinder or advance his cause. He knew if he didn't tend to his marriage he might lose what he really wanted. So, he chose (at least temporarily) to alter course.

In the story of Joe and Mary, Mary confronted Joe several times about what she felt was insensitivity and ruthlessness on his part in his treatment of Lisa. Joe denied his aggressiveness. He also successfully convinced Mary that what she felt in her gut was his aggressiveness was really conscientiousness, loyalty, and passionate fatherly concern. Joe wanted a daughter who got all A's. Mary stood in the way. Joe's denial was the tactic he used to remove Mary as an obstacle to what he wanted.

Selective Inattention (or selective attention)—This is when aggressors actively ignore the warnings, pleas, or wishes of others, and, in general refuse to pay attention to everything or anything that might distract them from pursuing their agenda. Often, the aggressor knows full well what you want from him when he starts to exhibit this "I don't want to hear it!" behavior. By using this tactic, the aggressor actively resists submitting himself to the tasks of paying attention to and refraining from the behavior you want him to change.

In the story of Jenny and Amanda, Jenny tried to tell Amanda she was losing privileges because she was behaving irresponsibly. But Amanda wouldn't listen. Her teachers tried to tell her what she needed to do to improve her grades but she didn't listen to them either. Actively listening to and heeding the suggestions of some-one else are, among other things, acts of submission. And, as you may remember from the story, Amanda is not a girl who submits easily. Determined to let nothing stand in her way, and convinced she had the manipulative skills to eventually "win" most of her power struggles with authority figures, Amanda closed her ears. She didn't see any need to listen. From her point of view, she would only have lost some power and control if she submitted herself to the guidance and direction offered by those whom she viewed as less powerful, clever and capable as herself.

Some children who have been labeled as having attention deficits are children who over-utilize selective attention as a manipulative device and a primary means of avoiding responsibility. These children show an incredible capacity to focus and maintain attention on any task or situation they find pleasurably stimulating, interesting, or in some other way, desirable. Yet, whenever they're asked to hear something they don't really want to hear or do something they'd rather not do, they will redirect their attention to almost anything else. This is especially true when an authority figure is giving them instruction or a directive. All they have to do is hear an admonition coming and they start fighting against it through inattention.

One of the most consistently positive experiences I've had working with manipulative people (especially children) is how well they seem to respond to being confronted about and dealt with appropriately when they use the tactic of selective inattention. This is particularly true when they are sincerely and strongly reinforced for choosing to pay attention to or invest themselves in something they'd rather not bother with at all. Often, manipulative children are dragged into a therapist's office by exasperated parents and they don't really want to talk or listen. I let them experience the utter boredom and discomfort of not engaging with them at all (by not talking to them and not actively listening to them, etc.) unless they are making direct eye contact with me and unless I observe clear signs that they are paying very deliberate attention. When I come to a subject they don't particularly like and they look away, I stop talking. When they turn back, make eye contact, and appear receptive, I resume. I call this technique *selective speaking*. A person making the effort to listen to what they'd rather not hear and to focus on topics they'd rather avoid altogether has earned my respect. I always try to acknowledge that and reinforce them for really listening. Their sense of self-respect is always enhanced when they acknowledge the value of this effort. Remember, it's impossible for a person to accept something and resist at the same time. So, when a person is deliberately tuning you out, there's no point in wasting your breath. When they stop resisting (fighting) and pay attention, you have a chance to be heard.

Rationalization—A rationalization is the excuse an aggressor makes for engaging in what they know is an inappropriate or harmful behavior. It can be an effective tactic, especially when the explanation or justification the aggressor offers makes just enough sense that any reasonably conscientious person is likely to fall for it. It's a powerful tactic because it not only serves to remove any internal resistance the aggressor might have about doing what they want to do (quieting any qualms of conscience they might have) but also to keep others off their back. If the aggressor can convince you they're justified in whatever they're doing, then they're freer to pursue their goals without interference.

In the story of little Lisa, Mary felt uneasy about the relentlessness with which Joe pursued his quest to make his daughter an obedient, all-A student once again. And, she was aware of Lisa's expressed desire to pursue counseling as a means of addressing and perhaps solving some of her problems. Although she felt uneasy about Joe's forcefulness and sensed the impact on her daughter, she allowed herself to become persuaded by his rationalizations that any concerned parent ought to know his daughter better than some relatively dispassionate outsider and that he was only doing his duty by doing as much as he possibly could to "help" his "little girl."

When a manipulator really wants to make headway with their rationalizations they'll be sure their excuses are combined with other effective tactics. For example, when Joe was "selling"

121

Mary on the justification for shoving his agenda down everyone's throat, he was also sending out subtle invitations for her to feel ashamed (*shaming* her for not being as "concerned" a parent as he was) as well as to feel guilty (guilt-tripping her) for not being as conscientious as he was pretending to be.

Diversion—A moving target is hard to hit. When we try to pin manipulators down or try to keep a discussion focused on a single issue or behavior we don't like, they're expert at knowing how to change the subject, dodge the issue or in some way throw us a curve. Magicians have long known that if they can successfully redirect your attention, you're likely to miss them slipping something into or out of their pocket. Manipulators use *distraction* and *diversion* techniques to keep the focus off of their behavior, move us off-track, and keep themselves free to promote their self-serving hidden agendas. Sometimes this can be very subtle. You may confront your manipulator on a very important issue only to find yourself minutes later wondering how you got on the topic you're talking about then.

In the story of Jenny and her daughter, Jenny asked Amanda about whether or not she had been turning in her homework. Rather than respond directly to the issue being addressed, Amanda diverted attention to her teacher's and classmates' treatment of her. Jenny allowed Amanda to steer her off track. She never got a straight answer to the question.

Another example of a diversion tactic can be found in the story of Don and Al. Al changed the subject when Don asked him if he had any plans to replace him. He focused on whether he was unhappy or not with Don's sales performance—as if that's what Don had asked him about in the first place. He never gave him a straight answer to a straight question (manipulators are notorious for this). He told him what he though would make Don feel less anxious and would steer him away from pursuing the matter any further. Al left feeling like he'd gotten an answer but all he really got was the "runaround."

Early in the current school year, I found it necessary to address my son's irresponsibility about doing his homework by making a rule that he bring his books home every night. One time I asked: "Did you bring your books home today?" His response was: "Guess what, Dad. Instead of tomorrow, we're not going to have our test until Friday." My question was simple and direct. His answer was deliberately evasive and diversionary. He knew that if he answered the question directly and honestly, he would have received a consequence for failing to bring his books home. By using diversion (and also offering a rationalization) he was already fighting with me to avoid that consequence. Whenever someone is not responding directly to an issue, you can safely assume that for some reason, they're trying to give you the slip.

Evasion—Closely related to diversion, this is a tactic by which a manipulator tries to avoid being cornered on an issue by giving rambling, irrelevant responses to a direct question or otherwise trying to skirt an issue. A subtle, but effective form of evasion is the deliberate use of **vagueness.** Covert-aggressives are adept at giving vague answers to the simplest, most direct questions. You have to have a sensitive ear for this. Sometimes the vagueness is not so pronounced and you think you have an answer when in fact you don't.

I once asked a patient if he had ever been diagnosed in the past with a substance abuse problem. He replied: "My wife took me to a place once, they talked to me a bit and they said I didn't have to come back." This was a response filled with evasion, vagueness, and lying by omission. There were grains of truth in what he said. But the whole story is a lot different. In fact, the man had been to a mental health center for an initial interview. His wife pressured him to go. He attended the initial evaluation session and was told by a counselor that he qualified for a substance abuse diagnosis. He was scheduled for follow-up group and individual therapy sessions. He failed to show up for most of his sessions, and after coming late to one group was chastised and told he probably shouldn't come back unless he was serious about getting help for his problem. What he wanted me to think when he made his first statement, however, was that someone evaluated him and then "they" (an example in itself of deliberate vagueness) gave him a clean bill of health.

Covert Intimidation – Aggressors frequently threaten their victims to keep them anxious, apprehensive and in a one-down position. They are adept at countering arguments with such passion and intensity that they effectively throw their opponents on the defensive. Covert-aggressive personalities primarily *intimidate* their victims by making *veiled* (subtle, indirect or implied) *threats*. This way, they throw others on the defensive without appearing overtly hostile or intimidating.

In the story of Mary Jane, her boss was well aware of how important it would be for her to get a good reference from him in order to secure another job. His implied threat to her was that he would foil her attempts to secure another job if she dared to expose him. As she reflected on many or her encounters with him during therapy sessions, Mary Jane eventually recalled several times her boss was subtly threatening. She realized it was probably no accident that he made comments about "how hard it is these days to find work" and how he was "always carefully considering the kind of recommendation" he would give her whenever she addressed the issue of a raise or expressed the slightest discomfort about some of his sexually perturbing behaviors. Because she really needed the work, Mary Jane was in a definite one-down position. Her boss's subtle threats to place her in an even weaker position kept her securely under his thumb.

As the last tactic discussed in this chapter will reveal, both overt and covert intimidation are effective manipulation tactics. But most cover-aggressive personalities prefer using covert-intimidation to get their way. *By not doing anything obviously threatening*, they can play an effective game of impression management. It's important for covert-aggressives to have their way with you but still look good.

Guilt-tripping—This is one of the covert-aggressive's two favorite weapons (the other is shaming) in the manipulation armory. It's a special kind of intimidation tactic. One thing that aggressive personalities know well is that other types of persons, especially neurotics, have very different consciences than they do. They also know that the hallmark qualities of a sound conscience are the capacities for guilt and shame. Manipulators are skilled at using what they know to be the greater conscientiousness of their victims as a means of keeping them in a self-doubting, anxious, and submissive position. The more conscientious the potential victim, the more effective guilt is as a weapon.

In the story of Janice and Bill, Bill knows how readily Janice feels guilty when she's not investing most of her time and energy tending to his and their children's needs. He used this knowledge to keep a hold on her when she was thinking of leaving. He used some milder guilt-tripping in his phone conversations when he mentioned how the kids were doing or how lonely he was. When those manipulations failed, he used the ultimate guilt-trip. What conscientious caretaker could stand to think of themselves as the cause of someone's death?

Aggressive personalities of all types use guilt-tripping so frequently and effectively as a manipulative tactic, that I believe it illustrates how fundamentally different in character they are compared to other (especially neurotic) personalities. All a manipulator has to do is suggest to the conscientious person that they don't care enough, are too selfish, etc., and that person immediately starts to feel bad. On the contrary, a conscientious person might try until they're blue in the face to get a manipulator (or any other aggressive personality or disordered character) to feel badly about a hurtful behavior, acknowledge responsibility, or admit wrongdoing, to absolutely no avail.

Shaming—This is the technique of using subtle sarcasm and put-downs as a means of increasing fear and self-doubt in others. Covert-aggressives use this tactic to make others feel inadequate or unworthy, and therefore, defer to them. It's an effective way to foster a continued sense of personal inadequacy in the weaker party, thereby allowing an aggressor to maintain a position of dominance.

When Joe loudly proclaimed any "good" parent would do just as he was doing to help Lisa, he subtly implied Mary would be a "bad" parent is she didn't attempt to do the same. He "invited" her to feel ashamed of herself. The tactic was effective. Mary eventually felt ashamed for taking a position that made it appear she didn't care enough about her own daughter. Even more doubtful of her worth as a person and a parent, Mary deferred to Joe, thus enabling him to retain a position of dominance over her.

Covert-aggressives are expert at using shaming tactics in the most subtle ways. Sometimes it can just be in the glances they give or the tone of voice they use. Using rhetorical comments, subtle sarcasm and other techniques, they can invite you to feel ashamed of yourself for even daring to challenge them. I remember how

Joe tried to shame me when I considered accepting the educational assessment performed by Lisa's school. He said something like: "I'm not sure what kind of doctor you are or just what kind of credentials you have, but I'm sure you'd agree that a youngster's grades wouldn't slip as much as Lisa's for no reason. You couldn't be entirely certain she didn't have a learning disability unless you did some testing, could you?" With those words, he "invited" me to feel ashamed of myself for not at least considering doing just as he asked. If I didn't have a suspicion about what he was up to, I might have accepted this invitation without a second thought.

Playing the Victim Role—This tactic involves portraying oneself as a victim of circumstance or someone else's behavior in order to gain sympathy, evoke compassion and thereby get something from another. One thing that covert-aggressive personalities count on is the fact that less calloused and hostile personalities usually can't stand to see anyone suffering. Therefore, the tactic is simple. Convince your victim you're suffering in some way, and they'll try to relieve your distress. One vulnerability of the conscientious, sensitive, and caring soul, is that it's easy to play on his or her sympathy. Could anyone be better at this tactic than Bill in the story of Janice and Bill? None of the other tactics Bill tried enticed Janice to come back. But seeing him lying in a hospital bed, apparently emotionally bruised and desperate, was more than Janice could bear.

In the story of Amanda and Jenny, Amanda was good at playing the victim role, too. She had her mother believing that she (Amanda) was the victim of extremely unfair treatment and the target of unwarranted hostility. I remember Jenny telling me: "Sometimes I think Amanda's wrong when she says her teacher hates her and I hate her. But what if that's what she really believes? Can I afford to be so firm with her if she believes in her heart that I hate her?" I remember telling Jenny: "Whether Amanda has come to believe her own distortions is almost irrelevant. She manipulates you because *you* believe that she believes it and allow that supposed belief to serve as an excuse for her undisciplined aggression."

Vilifying the Victim—This tactic is frequently used in conjunction with the tactic of playing the victim role. The aggressor uses this tactic to make it appear he is only responding (i.e. defending himself against) aggression on the part of the victim. It enables the aggressor to better put the victim on the defensive.

Returning again to the story of Jenny and Amanda, when Amanda accuses her mother of "hating" her and "always saying mean things" to her, she not only invites Jenny to feel like a "bully" herself, but simultaneously succeeds in "bullying" her into backing off. More than any other, the tactic of vilifying the victim is a powerful means of putting someone unconsciously on the defensive while simultaneously masking the aggressive intent and behavior of the person using the tactic.

Playing the Servant Role—Covert-aggressives use this tactic to cloak their self-serving agendas in the guise of service to a more noble cause. It's a common tactic but difficult to recognize. By pretending to be working hard on someone else's behalf, covert-aggressives conceal their own ambition, desire for power, and quest for a position of dominance over others.

In the story of James (the minister) and Jean, James appeared to many to be the tireless servant. He attended more activities than he needed to attend and did so eagerly. But if devoted service to those who needed him was his aim, how does one explain the degree to which James habitually neglected his family? As an aggressive personality, James submits himself to no one. The only master he serves is his own ambition.

Not only was playing the servant role an effective tactic for James, but also it's the cornerstone upon which corrupt ministerial empires of all types are built. A good example comes to mind in the recent true story of a well-known televangelist who locked himself up in a room in a purported display of "obedience" and "service" to God. He even portrayed himself as a willing sacrificial lamb who was prepared to be "taken by God" if he didn't do the Almighty's bidding and raise eight million dollars. He claimed he was a humble servant, merely heeding the Lord's will He was really fighting to save his substantial material empire.

Another recent scandal involving a televangelist resulted in his church's governance body censuring him for one year. But he told his congregation he couldn't stop his ministry because he had to be faithful to the Lord's will (God supposedly talked to him and told him not to quit). This minister was clearly being defiant of his church's established authority. Yet, he presented himself as a person being humbly submissive to the "highest" authority. One hallmark characteristic of covert-aggressive personalities is loudly professing subservience while fighting for dominance.

Seduction—Covert-aggressive personalities are adept at charming, praising, flattering or overtly supporting others in order to get them to lower their defenses and surrender their trust and loyalty. Covert-aggressives are also particularly aware that people who are to some extent emotionally needy and dependent (and that includes most people who aren't character-disordered) want approval, reassurance, and a sense of being valued and needed more than anything. Appearing to be attentive to these needs can be a manipulator's ticket to incredible power over others. Shady "gurus" like Jim Jones and David Koresh seemed to have refined this tactic to an art.

In the story of Al and Don, Al is the consummate seducer. He melts any resistance you might have to giving him your loyalty and confidence. He does this by giving you what he knows you need most. He knows you want to feel valued and important. So, he often tells you that you are. You don't find out how unimportant you *really* are to him until you turn out to be in his way.

Projecting the blame (blaming others)—Aggressive personalities are always looking for a way to shift the blame for their aggressive behavior. Covert-aggressives are not only skilled at finding scapegoats, they're expert at doing so in subtle, hard to detect ways.

In the case of Janice and Bill, Bill abusively drinks. Not only that, he knows—based on a long, long history—that when he drinks he becomes quite abusive in other ways. When Janice calls these things to his attention, he doesn't challenge her outright. He does, however, carefully "point out" how he only starts drinking when he's feeling "unsupported" by her and that he doesn't do the things she complains about unless he's been drinking. He doesn't say so directly, but Bill blames Janice and alcohol for his abusive behavior. His willingness to blame her for his abusive behavior is, in itself, an abusive act. This is further illustration that at the very moment aggressive personalities are engaging in the use of this or any other of the offensive tactics I've been discussing, they are in the act of aggressing.

Feigning Innocence—This is when the manipulator tries to convince you that any harm they did was unintentional, or that they really didn't do something they've been accused of doing. The tactic is designed to make you question your judgment and possibly your sanity. Sometimes, the tactic can be as subtle as a look of surprise or even a look of indignation on their face when they're confronted on an issue. Even the look is meant to have you second-guess whether or not you are justified in calling them on a problem behavior.

Feigning Ignorance or Confusion—Closely related to feigning innocence, this tactic is when the manipulator acts like he doesn't know what you're talking about or is confused about an important issue you're trying to bring to his attention. It's the manipulator's way of trying to get you to question your sanity by "playing dumb."

All of the various disturbed characters tend to use the tactics of feigning ignorance or confusion. This is a very effective way for them to veil their malevolent intentions. Remember, disturbed characters, most especially the various aggressive personalities, are very goal-oriented, agenda-driven individuals whose use of tactics is conscious, calculated, and deliberate. So, although they will frequently claim they "don't know" what you're talking about when you confront them or had no idea why they did what you found offensive, it's important that you don't buy into the notion that they're not fully aware.

Brandishing Anger—It might appear a bit odd or even inappropriate to cast the expression of anger as a manipulative power tactic. The conventional wisdom is that anger is an involuntary emotional response that precedes aggression. This is the basis for popular anger management programs. However, my experience (and that of other researchers) is that *a deliberate display of anger* can be a very calculated and effective tool of intimidation, coercion, and ultimately, manipulation. Moreover, when it comes to understanding aggressive personalities, it's a mistake to think that anger necessarily precedes aggression. Consider the aggressive driver. The person exceeding the speed limit by 25 m.p.h. to get from point A to point B is clearly in the aggressive mode of behavior. When that person is most likely to become angry is when someone enters the highway in front of them going 10 mph below the speed limit. In other words, frustrated aggression begets the anger. And, the aggressive driver may blow their horn, tailgate, and engage in all sorts of displays of rage and intimidation to get the driver ahead of them to move. Perhaps, they'll eventually find room to pass them. Then, all is right again with the world.

Aggressive personalities use overt displays of anger to intimidate and manipulate others. They're not angry to start. They just want what they want, and they get angry when denied. Then, they'll use whatever tactics will remove the obstacles in their way. Sometimes, the most effective tactic is brandishing sufficient emotional intensity and rage to shock another person into submission.

Gaslighting—In recent years, several authors have referred to *gaslighting* as one the more sinister ways the most manipulative covert-aggressors (i.e. psychopaths) disadvantage their victims. The term comes from the stage play and suspense film thriller of the 1930s, *Gas Light*, in which a conniving husband plots to get rid of his wife by convincing her she is losing her mind and belongs in a sanitarium. He makes subtle changes in her environment, including slowly and steadily dimming the flame on a gas lamp, then tries to convince her she is the only one who thinks these things are happening. But gaslighting is not just a special tactic only psychopaths use. Moreover, all the tactics covertly-aggressive personality types employ can create so much doubt in the minds of their manipulation targets that the victims no longer trust their own judgment and buy into the assertions of their manipulator, thus succumbing to their power and control.

As I've mentioned before, covert-aggression lies at the heart of most manipulation. "Dirty" fighters employ tactics that effectively conceal obvious aggressive intent on their part. The manipulation victim's gut tells them they're under attack or that someone is trying to get the better of them, and they intuitively go on the defensive. But because they can't find clear, direct, objective evidence for this, they doubt and question themselves and end up feeling more than a bit crazy. This is always the secret of effective manipulation. If the "target" were solidly convinced they were in the process of being done in, they'd more likely put up more resistance instead of capitulating. Manipulators know this. They win by getting the other person to doubt—and eventually, to back down, see things their way, give in, and ultimately, to allow themselves to be exploited or controlled. And if a manipulator also happens to be skilled in the art of "impression management"—displaying superficial charm and enjoying the capacity to make favorable impressions on others—those on the receiving end of their tactics are likely to feel even crazier. They might say to themselves: "Maybe I'm the one who's really off base. After all, everyone else seems to like them and also to see things their way." So, in a sense, almost all manipulative behavior produces the gaslighting effect to some degree, which is why in early editions of this book I didn't highlight it as a distinctive manipulation tactic.

Gaslighting can be intentional or incidental. That is, a manipulator can deliberately set out to make the other person feel crazy as a means of injuring or gaining undue influence and control over them, or a victim can be de facto gaslighted as result of how effective and convincing all of the manipulator's tactics have been. But whether it's done intentionally or incidentally, gaslighting always has the same effect. Sometimes just the apparent intensity and conviction a covert-aggressor displays when engaging in their charades can produce the gaslighting effect. When they're rightfully suspected and confronted, some manipulators don't just deny—they deny adamantly. And if they couple their vehement denial with other tactics like feigning righteous indignation (i.e. pretending they are truly and justifiably offended that their victim would suspect them of some dastardly behavior or intention), the gaslighting effect is enhanced. The script for this tactic is simple: when you're confronted on something you know will expose you for the unsavory character you are, act offended and hurt, appear unshaken and resolute, and question the very sanity of your accuser. It's a simple but often highly effective script.

The more tactics a manipulator combines, the more intense the gaslighting effect is likely to be. Anything manipulators do to get others to doubt themselves and their judgment can enhance the effect. But there are some personalities who, because of certain aspects of their own character, are not as susceptible to the technique. So when a manipulator senses the technique is having some effect but not to the optimal degree, there are some additional they can take: They can go on a real charm offensive to make the gaslighted victim feel even more isolated and alone with respect to the feelings and attitudes they harbor toward their abuser. They can also engage in a reality and history restructuring campaign, subtly coaching relatives and friends to remember things as happening the way they want them to be remembered and then pointing out to the person being gaslighted that they are the only person who remembers things differently. They'll curry favor and form alliances to make the target of the gaslighting feel isolated. Some professionals have offered various terms for these kinds of behavior, including a currently popular label: "street theater." But regardless of how these tactics are labeled, the intention and effect of them is always the same: Make the other person believe they are all alone in their beliefs and have no legitimate reason to feel what they sense in their heart or their gut to be true and you have them firmly under your influence and control.

Gaslighting is not an uncommon tactic. Character disturbed persons who serially philander but want to deep their spouses in the dark and maintain control in their relationships are particularly fond of this tactic. They use it to invite their relationship partners to view what might be some very justifiable mistrust on their part as pure "paranoia." And they often combine other tactics such as shaming, guilt-tripping, and feigning innocence/ignorance with their other gaslighting efforts so the person on the receiving end not only winds up feeling like they might indeed be out of their mind but also like they're the worst person on earth for daring to think the kinds of things they had been suspecting about their manipulator.

After questioning their perceptions, judgments, feelings, and even their sanity for so long, it's often quite difficult for victims of gaslighting to restore a balanced sense of self, even after leaving an abusive partner. Sadly, not only have many victims written me to share this very kind of experience but also many have reported being stymied in their rehabilitation when seeking help from a professional not familiar enough with such severe forms of emotional abuse and the traumatic impact it can have on a

George K. Simon, Jr., Ph.D.

person's psyche. Victims of prolonged or intense gaslighting often need specialized help. They don't just want reassurance they were never as "crazy" or wrong-headed about things as their manipulator made them feel. What they want more than mere validation (although the validation itself means a whole lot) is to feel they can more objectively, fairly, and reliably judge both their own character and the character of those with whom they might again forge a relationship. They want to be able to trust again (especially their own judgment), and to know when and how to safely trust. While trust is an important issue for all of us when it comes to our intimate relationships, for the victim of extreme forms of manipulation, especially gaslighting, restoring one's faith oneself and in human nature is a pivotal event.

I've presented the principal tactics that covert-aggressive use to manipulate and control others. They are not always easy to recognize. Although all aggressive personalities tend to use these tactics, covert-aggressives generally use them slickly, subtly and adeptly. Anyone dealing with a covertly aggressive person will need to heighten gut-level sensitivity to the use of these tactics if they're to avoid being taken in by them.

What's really important to recognize here is that when some-body uses these tactics frequently, you not only know what kind of character you're dealing with, but precisely because the tactics are both tools of manipulation as well as manifestations of resistance to change, you also know that they will engage in their problematic behaviors again. You can give up your fantasy that in time things will be different. Nothing will change until they decide to stop fighting and start accepting. As long as they're engaging in the tactics however, it's clear they don't intend to change.

REDEFINING THE TERMS OF ENGAGEMENT

The most fundamental rule of human engagement is that *the aggressor sets the rules*. This is because once attacked, weakened in position, or emotionally on the run, any victim of aggression (including covert-aggression) is always scrambling to establish a more favorable balance of power. So, it appears that any person willing to launch the "first strike" has already defined the initial terms of engagement.

It's impossible to deal effectively with anybody when you start out in a one-down position. So, if you want to avoid being victimized by covert-aggression, or any aggression for that matter, you must move quickly to redefine the terms of engagement. There are several things a person must do to ensure that the frequent contests of life are played on a level field. To guard against victimization, you must: be free of potentially harmful misconceptions about human nature and behavior; know how to correctly assess the character of others; have high self-awareness, especially regarding those aspects of your own character that might increase your vulnerability to manipulation; recognize and correctly label the tactics of manipulation and respond to them appropriately; and avoid fighting losing battles.

Observing these guidelines will help anyone maintain a position of power and strength in interpersonal relationships regardless of the power tactics an aggressive or covertly aggressive person might use.

Letting Go of Harmful Misconceptions

Covertly aggressive people are generally so good at their craft they don't need our help in pulling the wool over our eyes. But as mentioned several times before, many of our more traditional notions about human nature set us up to be manipulated and exploited. One very significant misconception is the belief that everyone is basically the same. This misconception is common because of the influence of traditional theories [of neurosis] and their premise that *everyone* is to some degree neurotic. So, it's extremely important to remember that disordered characters are very different from the average, functional, neurotic. As previously mentioned, they don't act the same way, and, as years of research has confirmed, they don't even think the same way. Aggressive personalities are also very different from most other personality types. They don't share the same world view or code of conduct. They're also not influenced or motivated by the same things. In fact, much of what we've been taught about why and how most people behave simply doesn't apply to aggressive personalities.

Becoming a Better Judge of Character

Anyone wanting to reliably avoid victimization needs to identify the people in their life with aggressive and covertly aggressive personality traits. Now, it's not necessary to perform a sophisticated clinical analysis in order to get a feel for someone's basic character. In the parable from which the title of this book is taken, Jesus says "by their fruits you shall know them" (or, "if it walks and talks like a duck,..") The manner by which they habitually interact with others defines aggressive and covert-aggressive personalities. So, if you're dealing with a person who always pushes to have their way, who always has to "win," always wants the upper hand, won't take "no" for an answer, etc., you can safely assume that you're dealing with a predominantly aggressive personality. If you're dealing with a person who rarely gives you a straight answer to a straight question, is always making excuses for doing hurtful things, tries to make you feel guilty, or uses any of the other tactics to throw you on the defensive and get their way, you can assume you're dealing with a person who—no matter what else he may be—is covertly aggressive.

Knowing Yourself Better

Any manipulator's real leverage is in knowing the character of his victim well enough to know how that person will likely respond to the tactics he uses. He may know the victim will give him the benefit of the doubt, buy his excuses, be hesitant to ascribe evil intention, etc. He may know how conscientious the individual is and how effective shame and guilt will be in getting him or her to back down. Manipulators generally take the time to scope out the characteristics and weaknesses of their victims.

If manipulators gain leverage by what they know about you, it only stands to reason that the more you know about yourself and the more you work to overcome your own vulnerabilities, the more leverage you gain in your dealings with them. When examining your own character, here are some important things to look for:

1. NAIVETÉ. You may be one of those individuals who finds it too hard to accept the notion that there really are people as cunning, devious, and ruthless as your gut tells you the manipulator in your life is. That is, you may even be prone to engage in "neurotic" denial. If you are, even when you're confronted with abundant evidence you're dealing with a ruthless conniver, you may refuse to believe it, reluctantly accepting reality only after being victimized too often.

2. OVER-CONSCIENTIOUSNESS. Ask yourself if you're one of those people who is much harder on themselves that anybody else. You might be the kind of person who is too willing to give a would-be manipulator the benefit of the doubt. When they do something to hurt you, you may be too ready to see their side of things and too willing to blame yourself when they go on the attack and throw you on the defensive.

3. LOW SELF-CONFIDENCE. You may be one of those persons who is overly self-doubting, or chronically unsure of your right to pursue your legitimate wants and needs. You may lack confidence about your ability to face conflicts directly and resolve them effectively. If so, you're likely to quit asserting yourself prematurely and also likely to go on the defensive too easily when challenged by an aggressive personality.

4. OVER-INTELLECTUALIZATION. You may be one of those persons who tries too hard to understand. If you're also one who assumes that people only do hurtful things when there's some legitimate, understandable reason, you might delude yourself into believing that uncovering and understanding all the reasons for your manipulator's behavior will be sufficient to make things different. Sometimes, by being overly focused on the possible reasons for a behavior, you may inadvertently excuse it. Other times, you might get so wrapped-up in trying to understand what's going on that you forget that someone is merely fighting to gain advantage over you and that you should be devoting your time and energy to taking necessary steps to protect and empower yourself. If you over-intellectualize, you'll likely have trouble accepting the simple philosophy that there are people in this world who fight too much, fight underhandedly, and for no other purpose than to get what they want.

5. EMOTIONAL DEPENDENCY. You may have submissive personality characteristics rooted in deep fears of independence and autonomy. If so, you might be attracted to the more confident-appearing, independent, aggressive personalities in the first place. After becoming involved in a relationship with them, you may also tend to let such people run over you out of fear that if you stand up to them you may be "abandoned" altogether. The more emotionally dependent you are on someone, the more vulnerable you are to being exploited and manipulated by them.

Even if you're not in some kind of relationship with a manipulator, recognizing and working to overcome any of the aforementioned character defects is a worthwhile enterprise.

But if you are in a relationship with a manipulative person, not doing so places you at high risk for victimization.

Knowing What To Expect and What To Do

You can expect manipulators to throw at you whatever it takes to gain advantage over you. Know all of the tactics by heart. Watch and listen carefully. Listen *for* not necessarily *to* what your manipulator says. Be constantly on the lookout for tactics. Label the tactics immediately when you detect them. Regardless of the kinds of tactics a manipulator is using, remember this fundamental rule: Don't be swayed by the tactics themselves. Reinforce the idea in your mind that the manipulator is merely fighting for something. Then, respond solely on the basis of what you legitimately want or need. Don't react instinctively and defensively to what they're doing. Take your own independent, assertive stand.

A mother recently told me how much a fool she felt after her son manipulated her into backing down on some consequences she set for his irresponsible behavior in school. When he said "I just can't take it anymore" and "Maybe, I should just go away" (playing the victim role, making a veiled threat), she said to herself: "He's hurting worse than I thought. Maybe I'm making his problems worse. Am I the bad guy? Maybe I need to back off." She didn't think: "He's fighting with me now to keep his freedom. He's pretending to be the one being hurt and trying to frighten me."

Avoiding Fighting Losing Battles

People who are frequently victimized by manipulators tend to be too confused, frustrated and depressed to think clearly or act rationally. The depression they experience results from the same behavior that I believe is a significant factor in most depressions. That is, whenever we persist at fighting a battle we can't possibly win, a sense of powerlessness and hopelessness ensues that eventually results in depression. The "losing battle" manipulation victims often fight is trying to make the manipulator change. They get caught in the trap of constantly trying to figure out just what to say or do to get their manipulator to behave differently. They invest considerable energy trying to make something happen that they haven't the power to make happen. Fighting this losing battle inevitably breeds anger, frustration, a sense of helplessness, and eventually, depression. Once depressed, manipulation victims don't have the presence of mind or the energy it takes to stand up for themselves.

Put Your Energy Where the Power Is

Making headway in conflicts with aggressive and covertly aggressive personalities (or, for that matter, any personality) can only happen when you're willing to invest your time and energy where you have unquestionable power: your own behavior. Besides, investing yourself in something in which you will necessarily experience success is exhilarating and confidence-building. The more confident and energized you are, the better your chances for achieving success in dealing with the problems at hand.

It's hard for some people to accept the notion that they must

144

take on the burden of changing their own behavior in order to improve their relationship with a manipulator. Generally speaking, people who've suffered a great deal at the hands of a covertly aggressive person are emotionally drained and have a lot of anger toward their manipulator. They don't relish the thought that it's they themselves who have to change. They want the manipulator to work for a change and they want them to "pay" for their misbehavior. Only when they begin to experience the first small victories that come from conducting themselves in more effective ways, do they begin to value the principle of investing themselves in the only arena in which they have absolute power—their own behavior.

Conducting oneself in relationships with covertly-aggressive people is never easy business. But there are some general rules that, if followed, can make life with them a whole lot easier. I call them tools of personal empowerment because they can help any-body maintain a position of greater strength in their interpersonal relationships. They are:

ACCEPT NO EXCUSES. Don't buy into any of the many reasons (rationalizations) someone may offer for aggressive, covertly aggressive behavior, or any other inappropriate behavior. If someone's behavior is wrong or harmful, the rationale they offer is *totally irrelevant*. The ends *never* justify the means. So, no matter how much an "explanation" for a problem behavior seems to make sense, ***don't accept it***. Remember that the person offering an excuse is trying to maintain a position from which they should be backing away. From the very moment they start

145

"explaining," they are *resisting submission* to the principle of civil conduct and trying to get you to cave in to their point of view. And because they are resisting submission to the principle, you can be certain they will engage in the problem behavior again.

Once you stop accepting excuses, you'll be better able to confront inappropriate behavior directly and label it for what it is. Let the manipulator know that although you respect his right to fight hard to convince you that you should condone their actions, you will not accept or be influenced by any excuses they offer. This will help you send a clear message that you won't tolerate the behavior in question.

In the story of Mary and Joe, Mary really believed in her heart that Joe's excessive demandingness was a problem. Yet, she was too wrapped-up in his rationalizations and too affected by his subtle shaming and guilt-tripping tactics to confront him on it directly. Eventually, she developed the confidence to stand up to him. She eventually told him something like: "Joe, I think you're asking too much of Lisa and I think it's cruel. I'm not supporting you on this any longer. It doesn't matter to me that you say you have good reasons for acting like you've been acting. In my opinion, you've gone too far."

In confronting him about his inflexibility and ruthlessness, Mary had appropriately labeled Joe's behavior as aggressive and harmful. By dismissing his "explanations" as irrelevant, she kept the focus on his inappropriate behavior. Keeping the issues clear, and not being swayed by the tactic of rationalization helped Mary to become more certain and assertive about her own position.

JUDGE ACTIONS, NOT INTENTIONS. Never try to "mind-read" or second-guess why somebody is doing something, especially when they're doing something hurtful. There's no way for you to really know, and in the end, it's irrelevant. Getting caught up in what might be going on in an aggressor's mind is a good way to get sidetracked from the really pertinent issue. Judge the behavior itself. If what a person does is harmful in some way, pay attention to and deal with that issue.

The importance of this principle can't be overstated. Remember, the tactics covert-aggressives use are effective tools of impression-management. They keep you second-guessing yourself about the true nature of the person you're dealing with. So, if you base your opinions on your assumptions about intentions or are swayed by the various tactics, you're going to be deceived about the character of the person with whom you're dealing. Behavior patterns alone provide the information you need to make sound judgments about character. And past behavior is the single most reliable predictor of future behavior.

When Jenny, from the story of Jenny and Amanda, first came to see me, she was always trying to figure out what Amanda meant or intended whenever her behavior was out of line. This was especially true when it came to Amanda's verbally assaultive behavior. I remember Jenny telling me: "When Amanda hollers at me and tells me she hates me, I don't think she really means to hurt me. I think she means she's hurting because she misses her daddy and there's no one else that she can dump her feelings on." Now, even though there turned out to be some truth in what Jenny said, it was irrelevant to the issue of Amanda's escalating pattern of overt and covert aggression. Jenny had inadvertently reinforced the notion that it was okay for Amanda to emotionally browbeat others into submission whenever there was something she wanted from them. Furthermore, by focusing her attention on whatever she speculated were Amanda's underlying intentions, Jenny failed to see Amanda as primarily aggressing against her. Failing to see the aggression in the tactics of another is always how one gets manipulated. Amanda and her mother eventually addressed and worked through many of the relevant issues Jenny speculated about. But that only happened after Amanda's pattern of undisciplined aggression was more firmly under control.

SET PERSONAL LIMITS. Becoming more empowered in interpersonal interactions necessarily involves setting two kinds of limits on behavior. First, you must decide what kinds of behavior you'll tolerate from another before taking some counter-action or deciding to disengage. Second, you must decide what action you're both willing and able to take in order to take better care of yourself.

In the story of Jean and James, Jean often felt like telling James she wouldn't continue to tolerate his neglect of his family, but she didn't. Not only didn't she set any reasonable limits on his behavior, but she also failed to set reasonable limits for her own. That is, she didn't make a decision about just how much of the inordinate burden for tending to the family's needs she was willing to continue taking upon herself. Jean eventually did set some limits on both counts. Even though fate lent a hand and James was transferred back to a less demanding post, Jean let James know she wouldn't support any future effort on his part to secure a position in the church's hierarchy unless he were clearly fulfilling his responsibilities as a husband and father. She also made it clear she would never again be manipulated into bearing a disproportionate share of the obligation to nurture their marriage and family life.

MAKE DIRECT REQUESTS. When asking for things, be clear about what you want. Use "I" statements. Avoid generalities. Be specific about what it is you dislike, expect, or want from the other person. Use phrases like: "I want you to..." or "I don't want you to... anymore."

In the story of Janice and Bill, Janice wanted some solitary time to get in touch with her feelings and evaluate the state of her marriage. But she didn't tell Bill exactly what she wanted from him. She might have said: "I want to have four weeks to myself. I don't want you to call me at all during that time. Call my mother if there are any real emergencies."

Making requests direct and specific has two payoffs. First, it gives a manipulator little room to distort (or claim they mis-understood) what you want or expect from them. Second, if you don't get a direct, reasonable response to a direct, reasonable request, you already know that the manipulator is fighting with you, plans not to cooperate, or is looking for some way to thwart you. This gives you valuable information for planning your next move.

ACCEPT ONLY DIRECT RESPONSES. Once you've made a clear, direct request, insist on a clear, direct answer. Whenever you don't get one, ask again. Don't do this in a hos-tile or threatening way, but respectfully assert the issue you raised is important and deserves to be forthrightly addressed.

In the story of Don and Al, Don meant to learn if there were any truth at all to the rumor that a new person would be coming on board who might pose a threat to his job security. But Don didn't directly and specifically address all the issues that concerned him and he didn't insist on direct responses from Al. For example, if he had asked Al directly if a new person were coming on board, anything short of a "yes" or "no" answer would have been a signal that for some reason, Al wanted to avoid the issue. Most direct, appropriate questions can be answered with a simple direct answer. If you get more than that, less than that, or something completely foreign to that, you can assume, at least to some degree, someone is trying to manipulate you.

STAY FOCUSED AND IN THE HERE AND NOW.

Focus on the issues at hand. Your manipulator will probably try to throw you offtrack with diversionary and evasion tactics. Don't let those tactics steer you away from the problem behavior you're trying to confront. You must make the effort to stay focused, regardless of the tactics thrown at you.

Don't bring up past issues or speculate about the future. Stay in the here and now. This is very important. No change takes place unless it takes place in the moment. Even if some change does take place, it may not last very long because old habits are hard to break. Stay focused on just what you want your aggressor to do differently at that very moment and don't let any diversionary tactics take you to another time and place.

Once, in my office, Jenny confronted Amanda about the abusive way she was talking to her. Amanda quickly brought up how Jenny had treated her badly just the other day. Not knowing what Amanda was talking about, and making the common mistake of considering Amanda's complaint as relevant, Jenny got sidetracked into a discussion of what she might have done or said the day before that upset Amanda. Before she knew it, Jenny forgot she had been confronting Amanda about her abusive manner of talking.

The time did come, however, when Jenny was better able to confront Amanda about her behavior at the very moment it occurred and to stay focused on the issue until it was resolved. One time, after Amanda had snapped at her mother, Jenny said "Amanda, I won't continue talking with you unless you change your tone of voice." To this Amanda shouted "But I *am* talking nice!," got a wounded look on her face, and began to play the victim role. Jenny, however, in the most assertive manner I can remember seeing her, responded "I'm going to step outside now for a few minutes.

151

I'll come back and see if you're willing to talk to me in a more civil way." Amanda then received a well-deserved time-out. When Jenny returned, Amanda was more civil.

The most salient point I could possibly make about the importance of staying in the here and now is that genuine change in the behavior of a disordered character always takes place in the moment their usual tactics are confronted. Only if a person demonstrates that they are willing to interrupt their usual manipulations, excuses, and other forms of responsibility-avoidance and display some more pro-social behavior, is there any reason for hope that they are changing for the better. Promises mean nothing. Wishful thinking is foolish. Only the willingness to change course at the time of confrontation (and not just one time, either) provides any reason to hope things will be different.

WHEN CONFRONTING AGGRESSIVE BEHAVIOR, KEEP THE WEIGHT OF RESPONSIBILITY ON THE AGGRESSOR. This may be the most important thing to remember. If you're confronting an aggressor (or any disordered character, for that matter) about some inappropriate behavior, keep the focus on whatever they did to injure, no matter what tactics they might use to throw the ball back into your court. Don't accept their attempts to shift blame or responsibility. Keep asking what they will do to correct their behavior. Ignore whatever rationalizations they might make and don't let them sidestep the issue. When someone is in the wrong, the burden for change must be on them. This can be done without subtle shaming, hostility, or provocation on your part. Just keep the focus on the behavior the other person needs to change.

For example, Jean might have confronted James directly about his neglect of his family. She might have said something like: "James, I want you to tell me what you're willing to do to better balance your investment in your career and your duty to this family." If James dodges the issue, or uses any of his favorite tactics, she should just come right back to the issue and focus on getting a commitment from him about what he will do to remedy the problem.

WHEN YOU CONFRONT, AVOID SARCASM, HOSTILITY, AND PUT-DOWNS. Aggressive personalities are always looking for an excuse to go to war. So, they will construe any sort of hostility as an "attack" and feel justified in launching an offensive. Besides, attacking their character "invites" them to use their favorite offensive tactics such as denial, selective inattention or blaming others. Don't back away from necessary confrontation, but be sure to confront in a manner that is up-front, yet non-aggressive. Focus only on the inappropriate behavior of the aggressor. Confronting without maligning or denigrating is not only an art but also a necessary skill in dealing effectively with manipulators.

AVOID MAKING THREATS. Making threats is always an attempt to manipulate others into changing their behavior while avoiding making assertive changes for oneself. Never threaten. Just take action. Be careful not to counter-aggress. Just do what you really need to protect yourself and secure your own needs.

153

Janice threatened to leave Bill several times. She did this less because she really intended to take action and more because she hoped the "threat" of leaving would shake Bill up enough that he might change (a manipulative tactic in itself). But Bill eventually came to expect these threats and began to discount the sincerity of them. Whenever he felt really threatened, he made counter-threats of his own in his typically subtle, covert ways. He was even willing to "threaten" suicide in response to Janice's apparently more serious threat of separation. In the end, his threat was the strongest and Janice gave in.

TAKE ACTION QUICKLY. A train without brakes rolling down a mountainside is easiest to stop when it just begins to roll. Once it gains momentum, it's too late to take effective action. A similar metaphor applies to aggressive personalities. They lack internal "brakes." Once they're in hot pursuit of their goals, it's hard to stop them. If you're going to successfully engage them, get a word in edgewise, or make any impact, then you need to act at the *first sign* that they're on the march. The minute you become aware that a tactic is being employed, be ready to confront it and respond to it. Move quickly to remove yourself from a one-down position and establish a more favorable balance of power. You'll have a better chance of not being run over and will send your manipulator the message that you are a force to contend.

SPEAK FOR YOURSELF. Use "I" statements and don't presume to speak for anyone else. Besides, using others as a "shield" broadcasts your insecurity. Deal with your "opponent" on a one-to-one basis. Have the courage to stand up for what *you* want openly and directly.

In the story of James the minister, Jean felt more comfortable pleading the case for support of her children with James than she did asking for what she needed for herself. By using her children as a shield she was also sending a message about her hesitancy to stand up for herself. It was precisely because James was aware of Jean's fear to assert her own needs that he knew he could manipulate her through his constant guilt-tripping and shaming.

MAKE REASONABLE AGREEMENTS. Make agreements that are appropriate, reliable, verifiable, and enforceable. Be as prepared to honor your end of the contract as you expect the person you're bargaining with to honor theirs. Be sure you don't make promises you can't keep and don't ask for something you know you're not likely to get or can't be sure your manipulator won't cheat you out of getting.

When you bargain with any aggressive personality, try to **propose as many win-win scenarios as you can**. Doing this is extremely important and requires creativity and a particular mind set.[27] But in my experience, it's perhaps the single most effective personal empowerment tool because it puts to constructive use the aggressive personality's determination to win. From an aggressor's point of view, there are only four types of encounters that they can have with you. The first is they win, you lose. This is the scenario they most relish. The second is you win, they lose. This is the situation they find most abhorrent and will fight you the hardest to prevent. The third situation is they lose, you lose, too. Aggressive personalities so detest losing, that if it's apparent they have to lose, they'll often do their best to see that you lose, too. As morbid as it is, this is essentially the scene that all too often plays out in the extremely conflicted relationships that end in murder-suicide. The fourth scenario is they win, you win, too. This is not as desirable a situation for the aggressor as the "they win, you lose" circumstance, but it's a highly tolerable second best choice.

Remember that an aggressive personality will do almost anything to avoid losing. So, once you've defined some terms and conditions by which the aggressor can have at least something they want, you're half way home. Seeking out and proposing as many ways as possible for both of you to get something out of doing things differently opens the door to a much less conflicted relationship with both aggressive and covert-aggressive personalities.

Jean might have said to James: "I know how much it means to you to possibly secure a seat on the elders' council, but I also need your time and emotional support. I'll support you in your efforts if you agree to take weekends off and spend time with the family two evenings a week." Covert-aggressive personality that he is, James will always be "looking for an angle" to increase the chances that he gets what he wants. This way, Jean offers a way for him to have it without losing what she needs.

BE PREPARED FOR CONSEQUENCES. Always remain aware of the covert-aggressive's determination to be the victor. This means that if, for any reason, they feel defeated, they're likely to try anything in order to regain the upper hand and a sense of vindication. It's important to be prepared for this possibility and to take appropriate action to protect yourself.

One way to prepare for consequences is to anticipate them (and sometimes to even predict them). Make a reasonable assessment of what the covert-aggressive could and might do. Mary Jane might anticipate her boss giving her an unfavorable reference if she should seek another job. She can take steps to protect herself. She can file a formal, confidential complaint with the appropriate state or federal agency. She can solicit testimonials from co-workers. She can even research the possibility of temporary employment with a firm not requiring prior experience in the event her boss makes a "preemptive strike" by firing her when he realizes what she's planning.

Another way to prepare for consequences is to secure a strong support system. There's increased safety in numbers. Janice could easily anticipate that Bill would do something to try and get her back, even if she wasn't sure just what he'd do. She might have found much support in Al-Anon, or a similar group. As a result, she may have gained sufficient emotional strength to withstand the guilt-tripping and the other manipulative tactics that Bill so effectively used on her.

BE HONEST WITH YOURSELF. Know and "own" your own agendas. Be sure of what your real needs and desires in any situation are. It's bad enough that you can never be sure what a manipulator is up to. But deceiving yourself about your own wants and needs can really put you in double jeopardy.

In the story of Janice and Bill, Janice's greatest needs are to feel valued and respected. These are the things that really drive her. And, having little or no respect for herself, she counts on the messages of approval she gets from others for her sense of self-worth. So, when Bill tells her he needs her, her kids need her, etc., she is easily manipulated. Bill knows how to play Janice like a violin. All he has to do is sound the note of "approval" and she responds.

In therapy, Janice became more aware of how much she needed approval. She also came to see how by constantly looking to others, especially Bill, for that sense of approval, she denied herself opportunities to develop self-respect. Many times, she ended up doing things to get or keep Bill's approval that she couldn't possibly be proud of afterward. There was the time she went back to him after catching him philandering. This was after he told her how much more she meant to him than anybody else and if she'd pay more attention to him he'd never have to go looking elsewhere. Another time she denied herself the opportunity to finish her higher education because he told her that even with the kids grown, it meant so much to him to have a "full time" wife and household manager. By the end of therapy, she realized that her behavior was a vicious circle of self-defeat. Constantly doing things that made her hate herself only increased her need for approval. She finally saw that Bill was attuned to this need and manipulated her over the years by appearing to give her approval whenever she did what he wanted her to do.

Empowered Living

Even if you understand and follow all of the rules for more effectively engaging manipulators, life with them is not likely to be easy. However, life with them can be more tolerable, and you can lessen your chances of being victimized, if you keep your awareness high about what they are really like, what to expect from them, and how to empower yourself. The following is a story of how a woman who, after several years in an abusive marriage, found both the courage and the tools to turn her life around.

Helen's Story

Helen was not sure just why she wanted to talk. After all, she'd done much thinking before arriving at her decision. But, as she put it, she needed to "validate" her feelings and to get some "reassurance" she was on a better track.

She told me she'd decided to separate from Matt, her husband of 15 years. She said the separation would be part of a plan. She would leave and pursue some personal goals without the usual daily "interference." In the meantime, she'd continue to have contact with him. If he proved himself willing and capable of making real and necessary changes, she might remain with him. If he proved unwilling or incapable of change, she would leave him for good. This arrangement would provide ample time for her to see if any changes Matt made were for real.

"I'm not sure he will ever change," Helen asserted, "but I know I have. I know I have power over my own behavior, and whether

I remain with him or not, I'll be doing a lot of things differently. For example," she continued, "because I'll know when he's trying to manipulate me, I'll stand my ground if I feel I need to. I won't let him push my guilt buttons or intimidate me with his subtle innuendos and threats. And, if I give in on something it will be because I want to, *not* because I feel pressured into it."

Helen spoke of all of the tactics that Matt used in order to get her to change her mind. "First, he tried the guilt-trip routine, talking about 15 years down the drain and how I was preparing to forsake a sacred promise. Then he tried shaming me, pointing out what our friends, family and neighbors would say. The payoff was when he played the victim role and tried to make me buy the idea that he is the one who gets "abused" because I'm always on his case!" Helen smiled as she insisted: "But I didn't buy any of it. Every time he pulled one of those tricks, I told him I knew what he was up to and that I wouldn't let the tactics work."

I asked Helen which of the tools we'd talked about to empower herself she found to be the most effective. She replied: "Two, mainly. First, I set my own personal limits by saying what things would have to be different if we were ever going to have a future together. Then I came up with that I think is a good win-win scenario. I told him I'd be there for him for the rest of our lives if he was willing to prove he's really changed by his behavior over a long period of time. You know, we've tried counseling many times in the past, but he's always dropped out saying things were 'my problem.' Now, I know that he needs to change and I know that he couldn't be serious about it unless he gets into therapy himself and sticks with it for a while. So, the ball is in his court! He knows what he needs to do and what I expect. I fully expect him to test my resolve. But I know I will hold my ground."

Fighting Fairly

Kelley, a middle-aged woman who had been dealing with a very manipulative son, gave me some valuable information about how she was able to restore a better balance of power in their relationship. I asked her what she found to be the most helpful part of therapy. She replied: "The most helpful thing was when you said: 'Pick the things you're willing to fight for.' That's been a real insight. I no longer think that I have to do battle every time. On the really important stuff, I hold my ground, no matter what he throws at me. I expect him to challenge and I don't get mad at him for it because I feel more confident about how to handle myself. But I pick my fights much more carefully now. I don't fuss or agonize about the stuff I'm sure to lose the battle over anyway. I just let it go. Maybe, I'm just letting go of the notion that I can control him. I set my limits and impose my own consequences. The rest is up to him."

Kelley also told me that even though struggles with her son seemed inevitable, the character of these "fights" had changed greatly. "We fight more openly and fairly, now. I tell him what I'm fighting for and I don't apologize for it. He fights too, but at least I know *when* he's fighting. It's so different knowing what's really going on between us and what to expect."

Kelley's words have rung true for so many of the people with whom I've worked. Once you really know what's going on in the relationships causing you trouble, how frequently people fight, in what ways they're likely to fight with you, what tactics to expect, how to respond to these maneuvers, how to take care of yourself, then, everything changes.

UNDISCIPLINED AGGRESSION IN A PERMISSIVE SOCIETY

The Social Environment and Human Aggression

Our aggressive tendencies and behaviors are not inherently evil. Throughout the greatest portion of man's evolutionary history, only the very strongest among us were able to overcome not only the threats we faced from other species but also from various tribes of our own kind competing for limited resources in the daily fight for survival. With the dawn of civilization, the need for aggression as a necessary instrument of human survival lessened considerably. But as mankind's long history of warfare illustrates, this basic human instinct is still very much with us and is likely to be for some time to come. Therefore, if we are to successfully advance in our social evolution, we will need to fashion cultural and environmental mechanisms that will aid us in the task of more effectively harnessing and managing our aggressive instincts.

The political, economic and cultural environments we live in have a lot of influence on how aggressive we are and how we express that aggression. For example, Communism purportedly began as a means to prevent personal ambition and greed (ram-pant individual aggression) from damaging the society as a whole. But through its systematic repression of the human spirit, this touted system "of the people" became one of the more tyrannical vehicles for covert-aggression (i.e. the wielding of considerable power and dominance over others under the guise of protecting the interests of the "proletariat"). Capitalism, in its "survival of the fittest" style of economic freedom, encourages a great deal of unbridled as well as channeled-aggression in the daily competition for personal wealth and financial security. But the system also encourages—even rewards—covert-aggression.

Employees of free-marketers know there is often no safety or security within the "dog-eat-dog" workplace. As a result, rather than *cooperate*, workers generally compete with one another for limited company resources, benefits and rewards. Sometimes, this competition is fair and disciplined, enabling the system to work quite well. In fact, fair and ardent competition is a key ingredient in the recipe for excellence. At other times, however, the competition is ruthless and accompanied by the under-handed, back-stabbing, dirty-tricking behaviors that are the hallmarks of covert-aggression. I am not one who discounts the value of good competition. But this kind of aggression has the potential to breed excellence only when the "fight" is conducted in a principled, responsible way. These days, I'm afraid there are too few individuals with the integrity of character to compete fairly. In the absence of a much-needed spiritual, ethical, and moral renewal, it is to our advantage to advocate cooperative as opposed to competitive principles.

Today's culture places such a premium on winning, and so little value on *how* we conduct the fight for personal success and dignity, that aggression against one another—

destructive, pointless aggression—is way out of control. The saying attributed to Vince Lombardi "Winning isn't everything, it's the only thing" doesn't just represent one man's personal philosophy, it's a reflection of modern cultural norms. There was a time when both amateur and professional sports served as key avenues for spirited young people to harness and channel their natural aggressive energies, build a sense of community through teamwork, and develop character by mastering self-discipline. These days, no one comes to games if the team isn't winning, personal show-boating by talented team athletes overshadows team effort, and unrestrained brawls break out at the slightest provocation.

Our country's founding fathers intended there to be fierce debate and competition in the arena of political ideas in order to keep a check on the power of government and to prevent any one party's ideology from overly dominating all others. Today, the fighting that goes on in the political world is also out of hand. What was supposed to be a spirited contest about critical issues is often a no-holds barred donnybrook between two opponents, each trying to decimate the other. And the fight that politicians wage is mostly about winning and securing or holding onto power. It's much less about striving to uphold principles or advance the country's security and prosperity. It's no wonder that so many covertly aggressive personalities find a home for themselves in the world of politics.

In my work with couples and families, I'm always dismayed at the amount of both overt and covert-aggression I witness and the destructive impact it has on relationships. Most especially, I'm troubled by the degree of covert-aggression I witness between persons who have divorced and are involved in custody disputes (battles). What people will do to get back at one another, punish one another, demean one another and destroy one another—all in the name of concern for the welfare of their children—never ceases to amaze me. In so many cases, the welfare of children is never really the issue. It's always about what either or both of the parties want (e.g., revenge, saving face, vindication, money, etc.) and to what lengths they are willing to go to get it.

In many arenas of life today—political, legal, corporate, athletic, personal relationships, etc.—we have become a nation of unscrupulous, undisciplined fighters, and we are greatly damaging ourselves and our society in the process. More than ever, we need to recover a guiding set of principles about how we must conduct the daily battle to survive, prosper, and succeed.

Learning to Be Responsible

If we are going to become a more principled, disciplined society, we will have to teach our children better. In Freud's time, helping children to be emotionally healthy had mostly to do with assisting them in overcoming their fears and insecurities. But these days, teaching children to be emotionally healthy has a lot more to do with helping them learn how to appropriately channel and discipline their aggressive tendencies and take up the burden of leading a socially responsible life.

Teaching children to manage their aggression is never an easy task and children with aggressive personality traits will likely resist submitting themselves to the civilizing influences to which we try to expose them. To ensure our children have a good chance of acquiring the self-discipline they need, it's important their parents teach them certain things about fighting:

First, parents must teach their children when it is and when it's not appropriate to fight. It takes a lot of effort to help a youngster see clearly when there really is a legitimate personal need, a moral value, or circumstance worth fighting for. There are also situations in which there may be no alternative except to fight, even physically, such as in a clear case of self-defense. Parents must also help children learn to recognize those times when there is truly no point in fighting at all.

Second, parents need to instruct and demonstrate to their children all of the possible ways to get the things they really need without fighting. They need to explain the benefits of exercising alternatives, illustrate what the alternatives are, and demonstrate how to use them. They need to teach the difference between fair, disciplined, constructive competition and destructive rivalry. Before they can teach their children the appropriate social coping skills, parents may need to heighten their own awareness about what such skills are and how to use them.

Third, parents need to help their children learn the difference between aggressiveness and assertiveness. They should be careful not to chastise their children for their spunk, feistiness, or willfulness per se. There is an old saying that a parent must succeed in "bending the will without breaking the spirit" of a child in order to effect positive discipline. This saying has great merit. Parents need to emphasize that although the innate aggressive tendencies in their children are not inherently bad, without appropriate discipline, they can lead to high levels of social conflict and failure. So, parents need to illustrate how going after what you want while demonstrating appropriate restraint and appropriate regard for the rights and needs of others leads to a greater degree of personal and social success in the long-run.

The importance of teaching children these lessons could not be more crucial. Inpatient psychiatric facilities in this country are bursting at the seams with young persons exhibiting significant disturbances of character. Regardless of what psychiatric diagnoses they may be given upon admission, the majority of these youngsters are brought to these facilities because of their completely undisciplined aggressive behavior.

Juvenile delinquency programs in almost every state are deluged daily with young persons whose overt aggression has brought them in conflict with the law and whose covert-aggression has gone unchecked for so long that they have become very skilled manipulators. We simply must do a better job of teaching our children when to fight, what alternatives are better than fighting, and how to fight fairly and responsibly when they really must fight. We must do these things if we're to do a better job of building character in our young people.

The Character Crisis

The drive for power, self-advancement, and dominance is in all of us to a greater or lesser degree. Unfortunately, in this land of virtually unlimited opportunity, there are growing numbers of character-disordered individuals trying to achieve these ends without doing the hard work necessary to secure them in a socially responsible and productive manner. So, we have individuals who instead of educating themselves and "fighting" fairly for a niche in the competitive marketplace, settle for violently competing with their brothers for control of the streets in their neighborhood. We also have individuals who, failing to prosper to the degree they desire in the established "system," ally with others in counter-culture groups, which, under the guise of commitment to some lofty ideals, wage war on the establishment. To a disheartening degree, we have become a nation of misguided, undisciplined fighters who are no longer united in a common cause of mutual advancement and prosperity but ensnarled in an "every man for himself" pursuit of power and gain. The biggest reason that our country as a whole is losing its once outstanding character is because there are fewer and fewer people of sound character inhabiting it.

A most disturbing trend has been emerging over the past several decades. Because truly pathological levels of neuroses have all but disappeared, and because character disturbance has become so commonplace, the social burden functional-level neurotics carry to make society work has increased dramatically. Meanwhile, the burden placed on character-disordered individuals who tend to shirk their social responsibilities anyway has dramatically decreased. The integrity of our society cannot be maintained if this trend continues much longer. The greatness of our nation's character can only be determined by the degree to which its citizens develop, maintain, and display character in their daily affairs.

The overburdening of those already carrying the burden of responsible social functioning is an outgrowth of another disturbing trend. That trend involves society's increasing reliance on laws, restrictions, and regulations to govern our conduct and to solve our social dysfunctions. There is an old adage that "you can't legislate morality." Although the saying is most often ignored or criticized as overly simplistic, it reflects a very basic truth. Persons of character don't need a law to dictate their moral conduct whereas persons of deficient character don't pay much attention to or respect the law.

Every time I went to one of my state's penal institutions to do training, perform an evaluation or consult, etc., I encountered a conspicuously placed, large sign that read "No firearms, drugs, tobacco products or illicit substances allowed beyond this point." I always found myself whimsically asking myself to whom the warning on the sign was directed. Was it directed toward those responsible souls who wouldn't dream of engaging in any of the activities banned by the sign? Then I would chuckle as I imagined a person who had come to the facility to trade and profit from distributing illegal substances noticing the sign and then turning around, head held down, and retreating to the car because he realized his intended act was forbidden.

Passing more laws, rules, and regulations is not the answer to our social ills and our character crisis. Such actions limit the freedom we cherish so dearly and that is responsible for so much of our prosperity. Further, people of flawed character will always find a way to get around any restriction we put into place. A moral, functional society really only results when people of integrity are the majority constituents.

Back in the '60s, there was a nationwide call to address the "underlying causes" of poverty and to eradicate it completely. People seemed outraged that in this land of plenty, many lacked even the most basic human necessities. There doesn't seem to be the same sense of outrage about the character crisis at the root of our societal dysfunction and there also appears no significant effort to address the problem directly. Still, I'm encouraged that even schools have begun to recognize the need for "character education," despite the sad commentary such programs make about the current status of the nuclear family and other traditional institutions that once fulfilled that responsibility.

Building Character and Living Responsibly

Character-building is the life-long process by which we develop the capacities to live responsibly among others, to do productive work, and, above all, to love. As Scott Peck notes, loving is not a feeling, an art or a state of mind. It's a behavior,[28] and precisely the behavior to which the two Great Commandments exhort us to commit ourselves. Bearing this in mind, I offer the following philosophy about developing the character necessary to love and live responsibly:

Even though we may begin life prisoners of our natural endowments and the circumstances under which we were raised, we cannot remain "victims" of our environmental influences forever. Eventually, we must all come to honest terms with ourselves. To know ourselves deeply, to fairly judge our strengths and weaknesses, to achieve true mastery over our basic instincts and innate tendencies, and to overcome both the inadequacies and traumatic influences of the environment that helped shape us are among life's greatest challenges. And ultimately, our rise to a life of integrity and merit can only come as the result of a full self-awakening. We must come to know ourselves as well as others, without prejudice, deceit or denial, and we must honestly face and reckon with all aspects of our character. Only then can we freely take on the burden of disciplining and improving ourselves for our own sake as well as for the sake of others. Making the free choice to take up this particular burden or "cross" is the true definition of love. And our willingness and commitment to carry this cross even unto our death are what open the door for us to a higher plane of existence.

ENDNOTES

1. Storr, A., Human Destructiveness, (Ballantine, 1991), pp. 7-17.

2. Storr, A., Human Destructiveness, (Ballantine, 1991), p. 21.

3. Adler, A., Understanding Human Nature, (Fawcett World Library, 1954), p. 178.

4. Jung, C. G., 1953, Collected Works of, Vol. 7, p.25. H. Read, M. Fordham and G. Adler, eds. New York: Pantheon.

5. Millon, T. Disorders of Personality, (Wiley-Interscience, 1981), p. 4.

6. Torrey, F., Freudian Fraud, (Harper Collins, 1992), p. 257.

7. Millon, T. Disorders of Personality, (Wiley-Interscience, 1981), p .4.

8. Millon, T. Disorders of Personality, (Wiley-Interscience, 1981), p. 4.

9. Millon, T. Disorders of Personality, (Wiley-Interscience, 1981), p. 6.

10. Millon, T. Disorders of Personality, (Wiley-Interscience, 1981), p. 91.

11. Peck, M. S., The Road Less Traveled, (Simon & Schuster, 1978), pp. 35-36.

12. Peck, M. S., The Road Less Traveled, (Simon & Schuster, 1978), pp. 35-36.

13. Jung, C. G., 1953, Collected Works of, Vol. 14, p. 168. H. Read, M. Fordham and G. Adler, eds. New York: Pantheon.

14. Millon, T. Modern Psychopathology, (W. B. Saunders, 1969), p. 261.

15. Millon, T. Disorders of Personality, (Wiley-Interscience, 1981) p. 91.

16. Millon, T. Disorders of Personality, (Wiley-Interscience, 1981), p. 182.

17. Keegan, D., Sinha, B. N., Merriman, J. E., & Shipley, C. Type A Behavior Pattern. Canadian Journal of Psychiatry, 1979, 24, 724-730.

18. Samenow, S. Inside the Criminal Mind, (Random House, 1984).

19. Millon, T. Modern Psychopathology, (W. B. Saunders, 1969), p. 260.

20. Bursten, B. The Manipulative Personality, Archives of General Psychiatry, 1972, p. 318.

21. Millon, T. Modern Psychopathology, (W. B. Saunders, 1969), p. 287.

22. Wetzler, S. Living with the Passive-Aggressive Man, (Simon & Schuster, 1992).

23. Peck, M.S., People of the Lie, (Simon & Schuster, 1983).

24. Meloy, Reid. The Psychopathic Personality. Presentation at Spring Conference, Arkansas Psychological Association.

25. Peck, M. S., People of the Lie, (Simon & Schuster, 1983), p. 66.

26. Peele, S., Diseasing of America, (Lexington Books, 1989).

27. Beale, L. & Fields, R. The Win-Win Way, Harcourt Brace Jovanovich, 1987, pp. 10-13.

28. Peck, M. S., The Road Less Traveled, (Simon & Schuster, 1978), pp. 116-118.

ABOUT THE AUTHOR

Dr. Simon received his Ph.D. in clinical psychology from Texas Tech University. Prior to his retirement from active practice a few years ago, he spent over 25 years gathering information about and working with manipulators, other disturbed characters and their victims, as well as writing, giving instructional seminars, and composing.

Dr. Simon is a sought-after speaker who has conducted hundreds of workshops and instructional seminars across the country. He has consulted with business organizations, civic institutions, and various agencies seeking his expertise on troublesome personalities and how to deal with them effectively. He has been consulted by other writers and filmmakers who have delved into the area of covert-aggression and has made appearances on national television networks such as CNN and Fox News Network as well as numerous regional TV and radio talk shows.

Dr. Simon is the author of two other bestsellers: *Character Disturbance* and *The Judas Syndrome*, and is the principal composer of *Anthem for the Millennium: America, My Home!*, which gained popularity after the September 11, 2001 attacks and has been heard by over one million persons in patriotic concerts across the country. He also hosts the weekly program Character Matters on UCY.TV. He and his wife of 33 years make their home near Little Rock, Arkansas.

Other books by George K. Simon, Jr., Ph.D.:

Character Disturbance:
The Phenomenon of Our Age

The Judas Syndrome

For ease of direct and/or bulk purchase of psychology books and
patriotic music by George K. Simon, Ph.D., please visit
www.parkhurstbrothers.com

Visit the publisher and author pages on Facebook
Facebook/George K. Simon, Ph.D.
Facebook/Parkhurst Brothers Publishers

Visit Dr. Simon's Manipulative People blog:
www.manipulative-people.com

Website:
www.drgeorgesimon.com